DOG eat DOG

DOG eat DOG

Confessions of a
tabloid journalist

Wensley Clarkson

FOURTH ESTATE · LONDON

First published in Great Britain in 1990 by
Fourth Estate Limited
113 Westbourne Grove
London W2 4UP

British Library Cataloguing in Publication Data
Clarkson, Wensley
Dog eat dog: confessions of a tabloid journalist.
I. Title
070.92

ISBN 1-872180-56-6

Typeset by York House Typographic Ltd, London W7
Printed and bound in Great Britain by
Bookcraft, Midsomer Norton, Avon

For Clare, Toby, Polly, Rosie and Fergus

CONTENTS

CONTENTS

ACKNOWLEDGEMENTS

The author wishes to thank P.J. Wilson and all the staff of the *Sunday Mirror;* also, former colleagues at the *Mail on Sunday;* and Piers Thompson for suggesting the book in the first place. Finally, he wishes to thank Clare for her lasting advice and encouragement.

PREFACE

I WAS A JOURNALIST IN FLEET STREET FOR TEN YEARS. Working as a reporter on a British tabloid newspaper meant that I covered many of the most widely publicised stories of the 1980s. It was a time when circulations were buoyant and the competition between tabloids was fierce. Reporters didn't hesitate to lie and cheat in the course of their 'duty'. The game and the stakes were often frighteningly high as they chased those rare 'exclusives'. Never before have so many hacks been after so many stories.

What I have tried to do here is provide an insight based on my own experiences into how journalists on the tabloids operate. I am not particularly proud of my journalistic exploits, though many gave me a great sense of achievement at the time. On occasions I definitely overstepped the mark. But I was young and keen and having a lot of fun along the way, in what seemed to me a glamorous and exciting world. Some of those experiences seem unreal when I look back on them, and I got into some situations that normal, hard-working citizens would no doubt find tasteless and unpleasant. But there is, and always will be, a fascination for the tabloids. People love to hate them but they also love to hear about what they have been up to.

I believe that the popular press will always have a vital role to play in society. It provides news in a lively and entertaining way for people who don't want to read one of the 'heavies', and I reckon tabloid news is better than no news.

In 1987 I left the safe environment of a full-time job on the *Sunday Mirror* to pursue a freelance career in TV and film production. But my departure was anything but acrimonious. Admittedly some of my colleagues thought I was crazy to give

up a full-time career to enter an even more precarious profession than tabloid journalism. But it was perfectly clear to me
that I had peaked in newspaper terms. I had had a great run for
my money, but all the chases and the ducking and diving no
longer appealed to me. Making a clean break seemed the most
sensible course.

I set out to write this book because even now, almost three
years after my departure from Fleet Street, people still seem to
enjoy hearing about my tabloid adventures. So here they are.

ONE

Don't Even Tell the Wife About This One

'WENSLEY, A WORD IN YOUR SHELL-LIKE PLEASE?'

It was this all-too-familiar request that plunged me into a story which would cause more tabloid chaos than anything else I was ever involved in during my career in the Street of Shame. It came from my ebullient News Editor on the *Sunday Mirror*, and was one of a number of call-signs I had learnt to regard with some misgivings, since it meant he was about to brief me on a dangerous mission. But then, Mr P.J. (Peter James but 'PJ' to everyone) Wilson was no ordinary News Editor – even by Fleet Street standards. As a reporter; he had helped expose Lord Lambton and Christine Keeler; and as a newspaper executive, he managed to make every mission sound as if it would bring about the downfall of a government at the very least. Sadly, that was not always the case, but it was often a very effective way of stoking up a reporter to get results. Phrases like, 'This is a brilliant one, mate, it'll make your name in Fleet Street' and 'We could get an award with this one' spring to mind immediately as classic PJ-isms.

But on this particularly quiet Tuesday afternoon, I didn't really mind what PJ had in store for me, as long as it got me out of the office. I was frankly allergic to sitting in the shabby grey *Sunday Mirror* newsroom. I became lethargic and prone to illness. Anyway, I was by now completely immune to PJ-isms. I knew his outrageous claims were just a wind-up to get people going, and I had grown to admire and respect PJ for the way he got the best out of his reporters. Sending newshounds on desperado adventures was part of his job.

As I walked over to his desk in the middle of the open plan newsroom on the fifth floor of the *Mirror*'s once palatial

Holborn Circus HQ, PJ leapt excitedly from his chair and beckoned me into his tiny 'private' office – known affectionately as the 'bollock box'. About six feet square, it was rarely used except when a reporter had submitted an extravagantly fraudulent expenses claim.

As I squeezed into the cramped executive chamber, I totted up my last expenses claim in my head. Had PJ spotted the £200 restaurant bill? Perhaps that £120 drinks claim for 'entertaining a contact' (otherwise known as a few rounds of champagne for all your mates in the Wine Press in Fleet Street) was too ambitious.

PJ turned to me with a suspicious-looking grin on his face. 'Relax, mate. I'm not going to give you a bollocking about your exes.'

I felt relieved. With a wife and kids to support I needed the money.

PJ went on: 'I've got a tip here that could make us world famous, mate.'

Now this is more like it, I thought to myself. Despite my long experience of his great sales patter, I knew PJ really meant business this time because, bizarrely enough, he was talking in a virtual whisper, as if the whole of Fleet Street might be listening in.

'This is a real cracker, but I don't want anyone knowing about it. Not even your missus,' uttered my esteemed News Editor. I was just crossing my fingers and hoping he'd eventually let his reporter in on this amazing story. I didn't much fancy working on a job without knowing where it might end. But then you have to allow for the eccentricities of News Editors on Fleet Street tabloids because it is a job that requires you to be the ultimate piggy in the middle. The shit flies in all directions on the popular newspapers of Britain, but somehow it always ends up hitting the News Editor full in the face. Whenever there is a disaster, it is the News Editor who is expected to mop up afterwards like a human sponge. That's on top of picking up the Editor's wife from a shopping trip at Harrods, and providing the front-page splash every Sunday. It is a highly stressful job

that most newspapermen and women with ambitions to become Editor go out of their way to avoid.

Most News Editors are lucky if they last more than two years
in the job. Many end up begging for demotion back into the
ranks of roving reporters. Life on the road is so much easier. If
you've got a splitting hangover, all you have to do is ring in to
the newsdesk from whatever story you're covering at the time.
No one can tell if someone is in a bad way over the phone. But
if you're the News Editor with a sore head, there is no escape
from the office – everyone can see you've got a hangover and
they don't all approve. Even newspaper offices have their
prudes. But none of these things ever seemed to worry P.J.
Wilson. He had an enviable ability to live for the moment. As a
News Editor you would think he'd always be covering himself
in case a major nightmare lay ahead, but that was most definitely not the PJ way. As one of life's true optimists, every story
he ever sent a reporter out to cover just had to be true – and, of
course, sensational.

There did tend to be some extraordinary results. Sometimes
he would send his hacks flying off in all directions to follow up
bizarre tips about such intriguing subjects as black magic
rituals in deepest Kent (strangely they were nearly always in
Kent or Essex) and gay policemen changing sex in Aldershot.
This follow-every-lead policy inevitably meant that once in a
while, when a hard news disaster story broke (plane crash,
bombing, whatever), PJ would be faced with an entirely empty
newsroom. But old pro that he was, PJ would then simply ring
around his vast army of freelancers (often local paper journalists) and send them off on what often turned out to be the
story of the week. Meanwhile his so-called star reporters were
getting abuse off witches in Sevenoaks or perfectly innocent
heterosexual members of the Hampshire Constabulary. The
young rookie plucked from obscurity to cover a major story
would end up getting a massive front-page byline while the
staff man got nothing. It did cause bitterness in the ranks, but it
worked. And since that was exactly how I got started in Fleet
Street, I tended not to complain.

3

PJ began to tell all about this latest 'world exclusive'. The subject was Prince Charles and his love life, which, to the frustration of the tabloids, appeared to be entirely platonic. In other words, his name was regularly linked with a bevy of beauties (as we say) but it had become clear, over the years, that he rarely laid a finger on them – or anything else for that matter. PJ went on to explain he'd been tipped off that the heir to our throne had secretly met a beautiful young teenager called Lady Diana Spencer on his official train as it stood in discreet railway sidings in a Wiltshire railway station. Charles was on Duchy of Cornwall business at the time, but, PJ and I agreed, that didn't mean he couldn't have a bit of fun on the side. According to PJ's source, he had even got her to come back on a second night.

'This is sensational, mate,' said PJ. For once it looked as if he could be right. Then he added, with a serious expression on his face: 'We're really going to have to do our homework on this one.'

Loosely translated, what PJ meant was: Make sure you get enough evidence to back the story or we'll be right in the shit.

As with most 'sensational' tabloid stories, there was plenty of legwork to be done. The tip had come from a Wiltshire freelancer and the first thing PJ wanted me to do was 'go and see him and make sure he's not telling us a pack of lies'.

My departure for the West of England was sudden – I'd had little more than thirty seconds' notice – but that was nothing new from PJ. He had this extraordinary habit of dispatching people to all four corners of the globe without a moment's hesitation. If they didn't have their bag already packed, too bad. Someone else would get the trip to paradise instead.

Driving eighty miles down the motorway was peanuts compared to many other off-the-cuff assignments. I remember one Wednesday walking into the office at 10.30 a.m. with little else on my mind other than scraping together enough receipts to put through my ever modest average £200 weekly expenses claim. Twenty minutes later, I was scrambling through the awful mass of holidaymakers at Gatwick Airport about to jump on a flight to Rio to try for a completely unrequested interview with the only RAF pilot captured by the Argentinians during the Falklands War. It was a disastrous mission as he refused even to give me the time of day throughout the eleven-hour flight back to London. Then, in the ultimate journalistic insult, he agreed to give a press conference to the assembled pack who'd sensibly decided to await his return at Gatwick rather than chase him half-way round the world. But worse was to come. I missed the whole interview because I was on the phone to the office telling them he had refused to talk to me. The only thing I managed to salvage from the whole fiasco was that ever since then I've been able – all too truthfully – to claim I once went on a day trip to Rio. With all this in mind, I wasn't in the least bit surprised to be hurtling down the M4 to the modest market town of Chippenham for a rendezvous with our man – a policeman turned freelance journalist – and a lot more besides.

PJ had yelled at me as I swept out of the office: 'We have to meet the informant. Get our man to take you to see him.' Rather irritatingly, the freelancer had insisted I meet him at his home rather than a pub – houses were much more difficult to find – and so it was I found myself encircling Chippenham's largest council estate looking for (and failing to find) the first link in this great 'world exclusive'. The estate was one of those sprawling, red-brick-built, early sixties job lots, and every road and every house looked exactly the same. All were shabby and unpainted and seemed to be subsiding into their poorly-constructed foundations.

After half-an-hour and countless blank replies from locals whom I asked directions from, I finally achieved my first (and probably last) success on the Royal Train Story, as it would soon be known. Number 23 Frogmore was not particularly distinctive, but it seemed extraordinary that people could not cope with being stopped in the street and asked directions to a house not two hundred yards away. Still, what's new?

A light tap on number 23 brought an instant response – the ferocious, high-velocity bark of a huge Alsatian. If there is one thing reporters and postmen have in common, it is a hatred of dogs. Postmen, though, only have to stick mail through a letterbox. Journalists have to risk being savaged when the front door is opened by the owner who, more often than not, is not that keen to see you. (At this point you may be thinking: So what a pity there aren't more dogs in the world.)

What really irritated me on this particular occasion was that I was risking life and limb just to call at the home of a so-called colleague. Despite my mood, I was shit scared of that dog and I told the freelancer so when he opened the door and asked incredulously, as dog owners always do, 'What's wrong? You're not scared of Jimbo. He wouldn't harm a fly.'

A dog that wouldn't harm a fly might kill a reporter. 'If you don't lock that fucking dog up, I'm not coming in and you can wave goodbye to this fucking story,' I told him, eyeing Jimbo in terror. So began my vital investigation into Prince Charles' love life.

'Come on in, old son.' He beckoned to me as if he was trying to persuade a herd of cows into a milking shed. His thick West Country brogue made him seem like one of those village worthies you often see wandering around country lanes or propping up the bar in the local. He was about six feet four and must have weighed in at around twenty stone, so I'll call him Man Mountain. He showed me through to his lounge where I gently sank into a draylon-covered settee. Immediately I realised I was sitting on something – quite what I didn't dare find out, in case it turned out to be Jimbo's favourite bone and he thought I was making a move for it.

'Like a cuppa Rosie Lee?' asked Man Mountain.

'Like a cuppa?' is a question that has always haunted Fleet Street, because there is a very real dilemma in that apparently harmless request. Do you accept the offer and risk picking up some awful illness? Or do you refuse it and risk offending the punter and possibly losing out on the story of the decade. Ambitious young scribes who will do anything for a scoop always take the disease-risk option, and I was definitely one of those. It has to be said that Fleet Street is littered with failed reporters who never had the bottle to accept that dodgy cuppa!

In this instance it shouldn't have mattered anyway since Man Mountain was supposed to be on my side – he was another journalist after all. However, instinct told me he might easily be offended, so I accepted his offer and tried to relax while he lumbered off in the direction of the kitchen.

As I sat and surveyed his lounge, I just couldn't help noticing the TV set perched precariously on a makeshift shelving unit made out of building bricks. That in itself might not seem all that unusual, but the fact that someone had thrown one of the aforementioned bricks through the TV screen did give me pause for thought. So this was the man who knew the intimate secrets of Prince Charles?

It was time to put all these rather disturbing distractions behind me and get down to the business at hand. As soon as my huge colleague had settled down with his tea, I got him to tell me the lot.

In rambling Wiltshire terminology he explained how a mate of his in the Wiltshire Special Branch had got talking to him in his local pub and told him about the two visits the teenaged Lady Diana Spencer had made to Charles' personal train. On consecutive evenings at around midnight, Man Mountain's friend claimed, she had arrived at the sidings and spent 'some hours' with Charles on board the royal crested carriage. As Man Mountain poured out his shock revelations the ever-present Jimbo whined continuously. It meant that every sentence was punctuated with: 'Shut up Jimbo, you bloody dog.' If only his Royal Highness had seen us. After at least a dozen such interruptions, I insisted the wretched hound was locked up in the nearest broom-cupboard. It proved the perfect way to muffle out his whining, but I must say I began to wonder if the dog knew more than he was letting on . . .

So far there was one important point that Man Mountain had failed to explain. Why did this friendly copper reveal such sensitive information? Why would a policeman spill the beans and risk his career and reputation? It couldn't be just because he liked Man Mountain.

When I probed him on this point the answer was so extraordinary it was entirely plausible.

'It's all down to shit, old son.'

What on earth was he on about? What has shit got to do with a royal romance, I thought.

'What are you on about?' I asked incredulously. I really began to wonder if Man Mountain had gone off his tree.

He looked embarrassed. I could tell he was about to tell me something that was in some way dirty by Wiltshire standards.

'Well, it's like this, you see,' said Mountain nervously fiddling with his mug of tea. 'My man – the copper – was on special duty on both evenings and he was right shocked when the train pulled out of the sidings next morning and two poor sods from British Rail had to clear up all the royal turds left on the tracks. It was right disgusting.'

I couldn't contain myself. I started to laugh out loud. Here we were, about to reveal Prince Charles as the Romeo we all so desperately wanted him to be, and the only reason the story had leaked out was because two railmen had to clear the royal shit off the tracks.

'Did the turds have the royal crest on them?' I joked. But Mountain didn't see the funny side of it. He was genuinely appalled.

Let me explain why this horrendous event even took place. All the royal family's train carriages were built in the fifties, when the old-fashioned method of lavatorial waste disposal was just to let it drop out of the bottom of the carriage – hence the sign requesting people not to use the flush with the train standing in a station. The problem was that no one had ever got around to converting royal carriages up to the standards of their InterCity cousins. Perhaps this was an entirely honourable effort on the part of the Royal Family not to waste taxpayers' money on modernising the rolling stock. However, they were all upgraded in the mid-eighties, probably for fear of another Royal Train style exposé.

I was tempted at this delicate stage to ask Man Mountain if his informant had taken photographs of the offending objects, but I resisted the temptation. But even without photographic evidence, I had to believe the story. After all, who on earth would bother making up a story about royal turds lying on a railway line in Wiltshire?

Soon Mountain and I were heading for a meeting with our police informant – probably one of the few people in Britain to have seen the Prince and Princess of Wales' turds (apart from their nannies, of course).

My friendly colleague was taking this story deadly seriously, even if I wasn't at that moment in time. Earlier he had absorbed every word of P.J. Wilson's telephone spiel: 'This is the big one mate. You'll be famous when this comes out.' As you know, PJ had insisted I meet our informant right from the start, but Man Mountain took some persuading. At first he said it would be impossible – until PJ explained to him over the phone that his fee for giving us the story would drop to nothing unless we met the copper.

I was somewhat bewildered when Mountain jumped into my car and said: 'Don't ask me where we are going or what his name is.' He was certainly keeping everything close to his chest. If it had been practical to blindfold me while driving to our rendezvous, he would have done so. Eventually we arrived at a shabby looking working men's type club on the outskirts of Chippenham. I was certain it was only a few miles from Mountain's house but it had taken us nearly an hour to get there. No doubt he wanted to make sure I would never again be able to find it. Very handy, I thought to myself.

Jimbo's master told me to wait in the car while he disappeared into the grey Victorian building. For ten minutes I waited patiently for him to return. Being a trained observer, I couldn't help but notice lots of latest registration middle-of-the-range cars with thick black rubber aerials parked around the premises. Two thick-set characters emerged from one

Vauxhall that arrived, and it soon dawned on me that we were actually at the police social club.

Man Mountain loomed out of a doorway and beckoned me in. Inside, the bar was thick with cigarette smoke. About thirty men were spread around the bar in little huddles. Virtually all of them were drinking that favourite policeman's tipple – a pint of lager in a straight glass. It has never ceased to amaze me how drinking and driving doesn't really seem to worry our boys in blue. When I was a rookie reporter in South London, I used to spend many afternoons at Wimbledon Police Station getting smashed out of my head with the local CID. Countless bottles of Scotch (as well as the obligatory lager) were consumed, yet all of them would happily then drive home to their families in Croydon.

Here I was about to share a drink with a local copper – just like old times. But before that happy event could happen, I had to overcome Man Mountain's increasingly eccentric behaviour. Firstly, he ordered me to buy myself a drink and wait. Naturally, I bought myself a pint of lager. I'm six feet one inch and was wearing an anorak at the time, so I reckoned that a suitable tipple would clinch the I'm-an-off-duty-cop look. It all seemed strangely cloak-and-dagger at this stage. Here I was buying myself a drink inside a police social club on the outskirts of Chippenham, and all I was trying to do was write a piece about the Queen's eldest son and his latest girlfriend. But as time passed it soon became clear that this business was more Inspector Clouseau than Dirty Harry. As I glanced over at Man Mountain, I'd already cast the Peter Sellers role. He was mumbling into the ear of a rather dull looking (even by police standards) officer dressed in a medium grey suit with medium grey shoes and a matching beard.

Without any warning Officer Ordinary moved towards me and I realised that at last I was about to meet my man – our informant, the man who'd seen those Windsor turds.

'Any mate of his is a mate of mine,' said he. I have to say I didn't consider myself a mate of Man Mountain, having only met him a few hours before. But I wasn't about to ruin the

10

scoop of the decade by splitting hairs, so I happily answered: 'Nice to meet you.' A strange silence then followed because I was genuinely stumped for conversation. I could hardly start things off by asking him about the state of the royal bowels, could I? It really is difficult to know what to say to someone who has decided to tell all because he was so appalled by the sight of a pair of royal turds. Luckily he broke the ice with an astonishingly frank outburst.

'It was definitely Prince Charles and that Lady Diana Spencer girl – randy old bugger!'

I was about to ask him how he knew when he turned on his heel, walked back to Man Mountain and re-started his former conversation. I was bemused. Perhaps I had offended him in some way? Maybe I didn't look him in the eyes properly? You know how suspicious policemen can be. One copper once told me that he would decide if someone was guilty from the way they looked at him. Man Mountain then moved towards me. I was about to find out what sin I had committed in the eyes of the law.

'He says that's your lot, mate,' said Jimbo's master.

I was stunned. Surely I hadn't come all this way and risked being torn limb from limb by Jimbo just to be told 'that's your lot'. How could I go away and produce a royal exclusive on the basis of about a dozen words provided by an un-named policeman in an un-named social club somewhere in Wiltshire.

This simply wasn't on and I told Mountain so. I grabbed him by the arm and said, 'What the fuck is he playing at? We need more than just that.' Our man in grey was obviously well versed in the art of lip-reading because he scribbled something down on a scrap of paper and called Mountain back to his end of the bar.

Meanwhile, little groups of policemen remained huddled together deep in conversation and blissfully unaware of the stilted exchange of information taking place behind their backs.

After handing Mountain the scrap of paper, he calmly walked away from the bar and sat down with a group of colleagues. Not one of them looked up at us. We might as well have not existed. It was now becoming painfully clear that my world-beating interview had come to an end. Mountain bounded over towards me and exclaimed, 'Come on. Let's go.' I tried half-heartedly to stop him pushing me in the direction of the door but I knew there was no point in arguing. My scoop seemed to have disappeared in the smoke of a nicotine-stained police social club.

Squeezing into the car next to me, Mountain flattened out the scrap of paper that had been crushed in his hand and dropped it in my lap. 'There's your proof. Her car registration number and his name and rank.'

Believe it or not, in Fleet Street terms that was enough. I knew I'd cracked it. Here it was, evidence to support Officer Ordinary's claim that Charles was secretly meeting a shy, gawky looking teenager for late-night love-ins on board the Royal Train. 'They'll go barmy when they see this,' one executive on the *Sunday Mirror* confided to me later.

The next stage in my mission to tell the nation the truth about Prince Charles and Lady Di was somewhat more mundane. I had to find a phone box and call PJ to give him the great news about my major breakthrough. That might sound like a simple task, but phone boxes have long been the bane of every tabloid hack's life. They're like pubs. They are never around when you really need them. And Chippenham was certainly not proving an exception to that rule.

Four seriously vandalised telephone boxes later, I finally found what appeared to be a functioning kiosk. I presumed it was working because a rather unhealthy looking seventeen-stone (at a guess, of course) West Country mama was bellowing down the mouthpiece to her son in Bristol. Another obvious problem with phone boxes is that other people are always using them for lengthy calls just when your career depends on getting in touch with your News Editor. I once interrupted a West Indian pimp as he yelled orders to one of his girls in a phone box in Paddington. He took immediate umbrage at my innocent request to make a 'very urgent call'. On reflection it

was a rather silly move on my part, because he leapt out of the
kiosk, thumped me in the face and kicked me to the ground
before returning to the box and explaining why it was essential
his girl performed French rather than straight sex. From that
moment onwards I decided that pure deception was the only
answer when trying to make a call in a public phone box. With
that method firmly in mind, I yanked open the tatty door of the
red kiosk in downtown Chippenham and yelled at the female
bumpkin: 'Police. I must use this phone immediately.' If only
I'd thought of that ruse in Paddington. Anyway, this hefty
creature looked suitably shaken by my presence. Maybe her
old man had just got time for housebreaking. She looked the
type as she pounded out of the seemingly tiny phone box.
Inside I could smell a marvellous blend of female sweat and
Yardley 'You're the Fire' perfume – the sort of thing you get for
Christmas in Chippenham. Even the receiver was covered in
wet, sticky perspiration. It really was a delightful place to be on
a cold November evening, but the main thing was that the trick
had worked.

It was now almost two hours since my meeting with the
informant – I could have flown by Robert Maxwell's own
helicopter to Holborn Circus and delivered the message in
person in less time. And I hadn't even got through yet. First of
all I had to persuade the operator to take a reverse charge call.
In Fleet Street you always reverse the charges. Phone calls are
not easy to list on expenses claims because the kiosks unfortunately don't supply receipts – the staple diet of all on-the-road
reporters.

By the time I'd managed to get through to HQ, it was gone
7.30 p.m. Of course, PJ and the rest of the staff of the *Sunday
Mirror* were already in the pub. In any normal job you would
have thought it reasonable to give up trying to contact your
boss and start heading home. But working as a journalist is
anything but normal. I knew I had to get through. There was no
way that P.J. Wilson would let me pull off any story until he'd
actually spoken to me. On one memorable occasion he made a
reporter drive three hundred miles back to the north of

England because the poor innocent hadn't checked in with him before heading home.

Finding PJ in a Fleet Street pub was no easy task – he could have been in any one of half-a-dozen hostelries in the area. But my first call would always be to the *Mirror*'s local, The Stab. Its real name was The White Horse, but it was known to all and sundry as The Stab (in the back). I can't imagine how it got its name . . .

Meanwhile, a steady queue of agitated looking locals had formed outside the phone box. Eventually The Stab phone answered – it must be the only pub in Britain where reverse charges calls are accepted. The familiar voice of a rival news-paper executive answered. There was a dreadful din of people in the background. The Stab was busy as usual. Voices – some familiar, some not – were shouting and swearing. Maybe some of them came from the increasingly rowdy crowd gathered outside the kiosk. Hurry up, for Christ's sake, I thought as I contemplated the lynch mob staring in at me. I yelled at the executive: 'Is P.J. Wilson there?' Silence reigned. 'Is PEE JAY WILL SUNN there?' When victory came it was sweet. 'Yeah, hang on a minute.'

In the background (but then again it might have been the foreground) I heard the nasty executive shrieking, 'PJ, one of your minions on the blower.' A definite chuckle then followed. 'Must be your royal man. Maybe he's cracked it already.'

I couldn't believe my ears. Just a few hours earlier PJ had told me not even to tell my missus. Now the whole of The Stab seemed to know what I was doing. Here I was in a shitty little phone box with a load of village idiot types about to publicly hang me because they were fed up with waiting for the phone and PJ had blown the whole fucking thing. In fact he had only mentioned a 'fantastic royal yarn' which could have been about anybody, but I was in a highly emotional mood. As far as I was concerned PJ had blown my exclusive to the whole bloody pub.

But then The Stab was without doubt the root of much evil within Mirror Group Newspapers. The main problem was that it was (and still is) actually inside the papers' Holborn tower block. That meant it was always jam-packed with scribes from sister papers, the *Daily Mirror* and *Sunday People*. In most firms, you don't compete with your own colleagues, but these two papers were our most bitter rivals. So bad was our relationship with the *Sunday People* in particular that I was once hauled before the Chairman following a notably crazy run-in with a comedian's widow whom I doorstep-interviewed while a rather naive (I thought) female reporter from the *People* sat inside having just signed the widow up for her exclusive story on life with Britain's top comic. 'Why can't you work in harmony with the *People*?' asked our Chairman. The fact is that both papers were after the same market, and competing with each other gave us an edge that other papers may have lacked.

Back in Chippenham the atmosphere was getting more tense by the second as I carried on trying to transmit my all points bulletin to The Stab. When PJ finally fought his way through the jostling crowd of hacks and grabbed the phone, his tone was as cheerful as ever. If only he knew what I was going through at the other end.

'Yes mate?' he uttered in a manner that left me in little doubt that he'd forgotten where I was. Obviously he hadn't heard the opposition's joke about me being on that royal story. Pity, really. He should listen more carefully to his drinking mates in future, I thought for one bitter moment. But it was impossible to be bad-tempered with PJ for long. Nothing seemed to phase him so what was the point in getting shirty? I decided to just carry on regardless and tell him about what was happening.

'Great developments down here, PJ,' I enthused. There was a long uncomfortable silence filled only by the loud voices of The Stab in the background – and of my friends outside the phone box.

'Sorry, mate, where are you?'

'I'm on the fucking Royal Train story, remember?'

'Of course.' He was trying his usual bluff now. 'I know what story you're on. I just wasn't sure exactly where you were.'

You might think that this temporary amnesia was brought about by the effects of drink. Nothing could be further from the truth in PJ's case. To start with he only drank halves of lager in very small quantities. But also it's a nightmare for a News Editor to remember the whereabouts of all his forty or fifty staff. I know, because I tried being a News Editor once.

PJ may have been momentarily confused at the start of our phone conversation, but as soon as I told him about my meeting with the informant he barked: 'Come back to London now.'

It was the worst response I could have hoped for. It was now well after eight in the evening, and I'd even earmarked a pretty little country hotel just outside Chippenham – prawn cocktail, T-bone, a selection of cheeses and a bottle of house plonk. Nothing too fancy, but the least I deserved after my long and arduous day. Now PJ had gone and ruined my plans in one foul swoop.

Back-tracking desperately, I muttered: 'But PJ, I might need to have another crack at the policeman.'

My effort was in vain and I knew it.

'You've got enough already. I've got to have you back in the office first thing, matey.'

My mistake had been ringing PJ too early in the evening. I should have waited until about midnight. Then a bleary-eyed PJ would have answered the phone and told me to stay overnight and come back first thing. But now he knew I had time to drive back to London and there was no way I could get away with an overnight stay in a hotel.

After fighting my way through the nasty pack of prospective phone callers outside my kiosk, I bade Man Mountain good-night and struggled back to London, prawns and steak no more than a dream.

I was in the office first thing the next morning, fresh and keen as ever and awaiting instructions from commander-in-chief PJ.

The great man himself was already at his desk and the moment he spotted me he rushed up and grabbed my arm.

'I've managed to swing it, mate.' I didn't know what he was on about. Maybe he'd got me that wages rise after all. Or perhaps I was going to get that company car he'd been promising me for the past six months.

'I've got exclusive use of the Chairman's penthouse flat for the whole week so we can run the story from there and no one will know what we're up to.'

What an extraordinary move, I thought. It was typical PJ, and in an odd sort of way it made good sense. God only knows how he persuaded the *Mirror*'s then Chairman to lend us his flat. For that matter, God may also know why the company needed a flat at all. But that was hardly a question I was going to bother asking in the circumstances.

Soon myself, PJ and another assistant were ensconced in the flat. It came complete with *Mirror* canteen waiter service and two king-sized double beds, rumoured to have been very popular with a number of high-ranking *Mirror* executives over the years.

The next three days were spent making careful checks to ensure our information in some way resembled the truth. In Fleet Street jargon, a 'careful check' means looking up someone's name in a telephone directory and ringing them up. The Royal Train scandal wasn't yet getting exceptional treatment, despite the sensitive nature of the story, although we did actually pull out copies of *The Times*' court circular to check that Charles' movements tallied with the dates in question. And they did.

The second half of the week was spent writing and re-writing a version of the story so that PJ could show our revered and much feared editor Bob Edwards a copy of what was to come. Bob (or Uncle Bob as he became known after Bob Maxwell – the Captain – took over) was a highly cautious man at the best of times, and PJ knew that only too well. Bob was proud of the fact he was in the *Guinness Book of Records* for being editor of more national newspapers than any other person. He was always immaculately turned out – some said he looked more like a film star than a newspaper editor, and *Private Eye* even hailed him as a Jeff Chandler lookalike (Chandler was apparently a big B-movie name in the fifties and sixties). Bob was always understandably reluctant to get involved in any risky stories.

Despite that, Bob could be quite a rogue when he wanted to be. He had a dry, sardonic sense of humour, and when his jokes got through they took some beating. I took him out for lunch once. Naturally I claimed the meal on expenses – 'entertaining a contact' I think I called it. Our conversation veered from incredibly intense opinions about the future of newspapers to the state of a beautiful brunette sitting on the opposite table – it was all most confusing for a young reporter like myself.

Bob knew when a story spelt trouble and PJ and I knew he'd be convinced that the Royal Train escapade was definitely in that category. He wanted it confirmed in triplicate before he would run it in the *Sunday Mirror*.

It was now Friday. The whole saga had kicked off in PJ's little office on the Tuesday. Now we had managed to bash out a cracking version of the story. To be honest, PJ had written the whole thing. It is widely believed that the name (byline) that appears on a story is that of the author of the piece. That is seldom the truth in the world of tabloids. One of the reasons why I managed to get into the Street of Shame at an early age was that I had no pride at all when it came to allowing others to re-write my copy. Prima-donnaish squabbles about artistic values are rightly confined to the heavier newspaper hacks.

Once, when I was on the *Mail on Sunday*, the legendary (and at the time of writing still Editor of the *Daily Mail*) Sir David English plonked himself down next to me in the newsroom and began typing away furiously. I was instantly impressed that such a larger-than-life figure should still feel the inclination to write copy in the paper's boiler-room. I couldn't resist leaning over to get a glimpse of the great man's literary output. As it happened, he was busily bashing out (completely re-writing) the first two pages of an article I had submitted to the News Editor some hours earlier. At the time I was astonished that he made no acknowledgement of my presence whatsoever. He knew I was sitting right next to him, but as far as he was concerned I had no cause to complain since his writing skills were about to earn me a huge front-page byline. I am certain that was neither the first nor the last time Sir David provided copy for his paper, and other tabloid Editors are the same. Imagine the uproar if that happened on the *Guardian*.

Anyway, our joint effort on the Royal Train was brilliant. It captured the tone of Prince Charles' meetings perfectly – or so we all thought at the time. For PJ and I slanted the article in a way that suggested late-night meetings of a lovey-dovey nature but definitely NOT involving sex. We even wrote in the story that Di left the train at one in the morning – as any respectable girl would – but a sub-editor deleted this, creating the innuendo that she stayed longer. We envisaged the couple holding hands and looking adoringly into each other's eyes – nothing more than that. We genuinely saw it as a meeting of two innocents slowly falling in love. We also knew that was the best way to convince Bob Edwards that he should publish. PJ looked positively delighted as he rushed off in the direction of the Editor's office to show him the finished product.

An hour later he returned. The look of elation had been replaced by that ever-so-familiar grey-faced expression that always haunted PJ after Bob Edwards had given him a hard time.

'We've got to firm this up properly or else he won't use it,' he said. 'We've got to get more proof. It's as simple as that.'

We had to devise a salvage operation that would satisfy Bob Edwards' natural tendency toward caution. That meant standing the story up in any way we could manage – and at high speed. There was no time for errors, and we'd reached a dangerous stage. Within minutes I was driving down the familiar route to Chippenham. This time I was in convoy with my assistant and a photographer. PJ had insisted that the only way to gather further evidence was to go back to 'the scene of the crime'. That meant a mad dash to the railway sidings to interview railmen, villagers and local bobbies – or anyone who might have seen something on those two crucial nights.

It was dark by the time we got to the Chippenham area, and my assistant wasn't in the best of moods. He had been forced to scrap a date with a new girlfriend – as far as he was concerned, PJ had ruined his lovelife and he was pissed off about it. He was one of those classic Fleet Street victims who cannot sustain a relationship because they keep being sent off on wild goose chases at incredibly short notice. He obviously felt the story was a waste of time, and on top of that it was difficult for him to accept that I was in charge of the operation. Less than a year earlier, I had been a freelance reporter who helped staff like him on stories. Now he was working under me and he didn't like it one bit.

We arrived at the village near the sidings and agreed to split up and start sweeping the Wiltshire countryside for new witnesses. It really was needle-in-a-haystack time. We went our separate ways and arranged to meet at ten in the evening at a nearby hotel. At least I'll get my prawns, steak and plonk, I thought.

There was one problem with this arrangement: neither of us would know until ten how the other one had got on. This was highly risky because it meant that whoever dug up a good witness first would get on the phone immediately to PJ – a natural piece of one-upmanship. No doubt he would also add to PJ that he hadn't seen the other reporter for hours. There is nothing more vicious than the rivalry between reporters on the *same* paper. Often two staffers are sent out to cover the same story without knowing of each other's existence – it's a kind of insurance. I remember once a so-called star reporter (albeit a lazy one) was sent on a doorstep. He rang in to the news desk and said nothing was happening, so his paper dispatched a much hungrier scribe who turned up on the scene and grabbed an interview with the subject of the story. Meanwhile our star man was nowhere to be seen. He had given up hanging around in the cold hours earlier and retired to a nearby hostelry for a pint before slipping home. Having being told there was no sign of his star man, the News Editor had a hunch and rang his home. Guess who answers the phone? What an idiot. He was never sent on a decent foreign assignment again, which was the News Editor's own special form of punishment.

Back in the wilds of Wiltshire, we both somehow managed to dig up new witnesses to the Royal Love Train scandal. It must have been most satisfying for PJ – his plan had worked perfectly. I found a signalboxman who remembered seeing Lady Diana's car and gave a perfect description; and my assistant discovered a villager who remembered seeing temporary telephone lines being installed by the railway sidings at the time of the royal visit. It was standard security practice whenever a Royal Train parked in sidings to link it up with extra telephone lines.

'It's in the bag, mate,' exclaimed PJ, back on his old form. This time I had deliberately avoided ringing him until late because I was determined to realise my simple dream of prawn, steak *et al*. An uneventful evening followed. I had a row about journalistic ethics with my assistant. That was nothing new.

Next morning I was up early and steaming back along the motorway to London.

When I strolled back into *Mirror* Towers it was after nine but there wasn't a soul in the newsroom so I grabbed my customary canteen Saturday morning treat of a fatty bacon sandwich filled with Holborn's finest brown sauce. At that time of a Saturday morning, it becomes obvious why most Sunday newspapers are filled with articles from the previous week. Quite simply, nothing much happens on Saturdays. Yet there is still the 'It will happen one day' lobby who remain convinced that big stories do break on a Saturday. Rather irritatingly, they are proved correct about four or five times a year, but it still seems a waste of the others to spend them in a dusty and deserted office.

To counteract the tedium, every Saturday the *Sunday Mirror* moves its news operation into the *Daily Mirror*'s vast newsroom – a tatty open plan area with an impressive array of clocks showing the times at different major cities around the world. The only problem is that none of them ever worked in living memory, probably because most tabloid journalists neither know nor care what time it is in Tokyo or New York, or anywhere outside Britain for that matter.

Circulation of the *Daily Mirror* was nose-diving at this time, and most *Daily* reporters spent more time in The Stab than anywhere else. At one stage there was a rumour that the manager had agreed to have an internal switchboard behind the bar. As was always the case on a Saturday morning, the *Daily* news area resembled a tacky sixties style dosshouse, with virtually every desk littered with empty spirit bottles and crushed beer cans. Often we would find a comatose reporter lying sprawled across a row of desks.

On this particular morning there were no collapsed hacks but the usual selection of used distillers' accessories. Eventually PJ bounced in, as full of the joys of spring (well, it was November actually) as ever. First thing every day, he always behaved as if he didn't have a care in the world. On this occasion I thought to myself: Give it time, old mate, give it time . . . But the morning passed without incident. The story was written and Bob Edwards seemed convinced it was worth running. But we still had another twelve long hours until the paper went out.

I just sat back and gossiped with some of the other reporters on duty that day. Gossip is an essential ingredient of life inside as well as outside the Street of Shame. I'm not talking about the sort of stuff that gets published in the tabloids, I mean the inside info on other journalists' private lives. Who's knocking off whom? Why is the Editor seeing a psychiatrist? Who had a punch-up in The Stab? Such fascinating subjects, and much more besides, are always well covered on a quiet, newsless Saturday. With the paper virtually full already, there is little a reporter can do other than wait for a disaster – and gossip. Hard news in Sunday papers is a joke much of the time in any case. Most of the contents are written days, if not weeks, beforehand, and most of the stories are just follow-ups of items that have already appeared in the previous week's daily papers.

As lunchtime approached, the lull-before-the-storm feeling

got too much for me, so I decided to take the only sensible
option available – a visit to The Stab. While a part of me was
desperately anxious to see the story in print, another part had
become rather bored with the Royal Train scandal. I felt, quite
simply, that I had milked it for all it was worth and I couldn't
wait to get started on another story. Little did I know . . .

One of my biggest problems was that I always tended to lack
stamina when it came to long-running stories. In a perfect
world, I liked to spend no more than a couple of days on an
assignment, write it, and then never touch the subject again. I
especially hated doing 'campaigns'. I'll never forget Bob
Edwards' great brainchild – the *Sunday Mirror* glow-worm
campaign. This highly unlikely piece of journalism involved
giving away little badges that glowed in the dark to schoolchildren out on the roads during the dark winter months. It was
without doubt an admirable attempt to reduce the number of
tragic accidents involving schoolkids on the streets of Britain,
but it so nearly sparked off a number of near arrests when well-
meaning teams of *Sunday Mirror* reporters were assigned the
arduous task of hanging around school gates to hand out these
badges to young children.

Not surprisingly, the sight of tatty, raincoated hacks loitering
outside schools at the end of class created some potentially
ugly incidents between concerned parents and 'those dirty old
men trying to lure our children with the offer of a free badge'.
The campaign went on *literally* for years and covering it
became the most dreaded task of every reporter on the paper.

Back in The Stab, life was particularly uneventful, although
by the time I emerged I could have done with one of those
useful little glow-worms to help guide me back through the
Mirror's darkened corridors to the newsroom. But I was going
to need more than just a toy that glowed in the dark to see me
through the Royal Train saga.

'Quick, mate, I need a word,' shouted PJ across the room in
roughly my direction. We sat down at two empty desks at the
back of the sparsely populated newsroom.

'Listen mate. We have got to try and stand this story up

properly.' I couldn't believe what I was hearing. 'The Editor has got really worried and we've got to get more evidence.'

'But I thought . . . ' I realised there was no point in continuing. There was a panic on and that was that.

'You've got to ring up the house where we think this Lady Diana Spencer stayed on one of those nights and find out if she was really there.'

You might well wonder why hadn't we done this anyway. The answer is quite simple. I had earlier convinced PJ that if we made inquiries in that direction we might end up alerting Buckingham Palace to what we were up to. The Palace might then issue a statement that would pre-empt our world exclusive. It's a standard tabloid tactic not to seek confirmation of a royal story from Buckingham Palace – and has been ever since the early seventies, when the Palace had denied rumours of a romance between Princess Anne and Mark Phillips when in fact they were about to marry. But now PJ was adamant that I ring the home of the Parker-Bowles family, where we understood Diana had been staying.

'The Editor says we don't have enough to run it,' said PJ. Whenever a News Editor has a problem with his boss, he always refers to him as the Editor, never by his actual name. PJ was obviously well up against it.

I did as I was asked. I thought it was a crazy thing to do but I wanted to help PJ. A lot of reporters would have sneered at the very idea of such a move, but I wasn't like that. My biggest fear was that someone at the Parker-Bowles home would deny the story outright and we'd have to take it out of the paper. I was as hungry as ever for that front-page byline I knew would accompany the story.

But, typical of PJ's luck, someone was in and they gave us what we wanted. A maid answered and, without saying who I was, I asked if Lady Diana was still staying at the house. Incredibly, the maid told me she had stayed the previous Wednesday night (one of the days in question). That was all I needed to prove that old Man Mountain's police informant was spot on. When I relayed this info to PJ he was cock-a-hoop. The story now seemed to be signed, sealed and delivered and, since it was around six in the evening by this time, we gracefully retired to The Stab to continue lunch.

We were just supping at our first drink in at least an hour when I noticed the happy expression on PJ's face disappear. He had just thought of some unseen problem, I could tell. Here we go again . . .

PJ had decided that once the other Sunday papers' first editions were out – at around 7.30 – we should call the Palace and ask for a comment on our Royal Train exclusive on the front page. I was slightly baffled. Why ring them after the paper came out? 'Just in case they admit it. Then we'll have even more evidence to put in the later editions,' explained PJ. Most Sunday papers have at least five editions through Saturday night and into early morning. The first editions travel the furthest to places like Wales and Cornwall; by the time the London editions come out on Sunday morning, they have usually 'stolen' some of each other's best stories. The other – and most important – piece of crazy logic behind PJ's decision to ring the Palace was that if there was any comeback on the story then at least we would have given the Palace a chance to confirm or deny it. We knew they would just say 'No comment', but we had to give them that chance.

The paper came out with the story all over the front page: ROYAL LOVE TRAIN. It was great tabloid stuff and the moment the paper dropped I rang the Palace as instructed by PJ. Naturally they refused to comment on the whole story, but we had done our duty.

I drove home later that night with PJ's congratulations ringing in my ears. Bob Edwards had remained behind the closed doors of his office as usual – a wise move as things turned out.

Sunday at home was tense. I was still unwinding from a strenuous week and it was only by about late afternoon that I began to behave in anything approaching a normal fashion. I was knackered, and suffering from a severe bout of Royal Trainitis. But there was still plenty more of it about.

Sunday was the one day in the week when PJ *et al* very rarely rang, so usually I had to endure a full day of domestic bliss from which there was no escape. Writs and complaints about stories seldom reached my ears until the following day. That meant I could either sit and worry myself silly about some inevitable complaint, or put the whole rat-race out of my mind. I tended to try for the latter approach.

Monday – not in the least bit surprisingly – did indeed prove to be rather eventful. The first health warning came when I opened the tabloids. The Palace was after our blood. Every single paper – including the heavyweights – ran denials from Buckingham Palace. Essentially, they were saying the Royal Train story was completely untrue. The dogs were after us and were clearly enjoying pulling my story to bits. Dog does eat dog in Fleet Street, and it can hurt.

I didn't know what to do, so I did nothing. I knew PJ and half of Fleet Street would be on the phone soon enough, so I decided to try and squeeze in a little DIY. I'd promised solemnly the previous day I would put up six shelves. I knew in my heart of hearts it was going to be a battle against time.

I had just drilled two holes in the wall with my latest birthday present – a Black and Decker power drill – and was about to screw a baton to the wall when the phone rang. I have to admit that on Mondays I often didn't answer the phone in case it was PJ about to try and send me in pursuit of some madcap story that would most likely end up in the bin by Wednesday.

But despite all the warning signs I knew so well, I felt the urge to answer that phone. Surprise, surprise, it was the redoubtable P.J. Wilson.

'Hello, mate. Look, we're right in the shit. Have you seen the papers?'

I felt like saying no and putting the phone down, but I didn't have the bottle.

'Yes.'

'Well, the Editor has been on and he's furious. He's going to ring you. We'd better make sure we have that story airtight.'

A wave of naivety came over me. 'What's the problem, PJ?'

'The problem is that bloody Prince Charles has got his Press Secretary to send the Editor a hand-delivered letter, and you don't need me to tell you what it says.'

'Jesus Christ. What do we do?'

'Stay calm, mate. We've got to look after each other.'

I felt like a bent copper trying to make sure all the evidence tallied as PJ rehearsed me on what I should say and not say when the Editor rang. If he sensed any doubt in my voice, my career would probably be over very swiftly.

At the end of the conversation, PJ said: 'We're both right on the line here mate. Watch your back.'

It was a chilling warning in the circumstances, but I was surprisingly unworried by this rather ominous turn of events. In the past, I had had many sleepless nights after getting up to all sorts of jiggery-pokery in the name of Fleet Street, but at least on this occasion I knew that I wasn't facing the firing line alone.

So, in a fairly calm mood all things considered, I returned to my DIY efforts. I had a job to do and I was determined to get it done. My screwdriver was perfectly positioned in the head of the screw when . . . the phone rang. It was my Editor Bob Edwards.

'Has PJ rung you?'

'Yes, Bob.'

'Wensley, are you absolutely certain it is true?'

Hmmm, I thought. This sounds like the ultimate professional buck pass. But then what else could I say. 'Of course it's true, Bob. I stand one hundred per cent behind the story, and I know PJ does as well.'

I was really getting into the swing of things now. I was even enjoying it. For the first time, I'd started calling our revered editor Bob. It was marvellous. He was even ringing me at home on my day off. How many reporters can claim that happens to them? For some odd reason the mounting royal crisis was the last thing on my mind. I stuck rigidly to my guns during further cross examination from Bob. I refused to concede any flaws in the article. It was the best way to operate – ride the storm.

Eventually he gave up his minor inquisition and bid a fond farewell.

I returned to my trusty screwdriver. Another twist (or maybe two) and . . . the phone rang. It was Editor Bob again.

'Sorry to trouble you again' – he is obviously not in the least bit sorry – 'but our lawyer is with me and he wants to ask a few questions.'

All newspapers have their own in-house lawyers. They are supposed to read every single word in the paper before it is published – but the writs still fly around despite this apparent preventative move. The problem is that tabloid lawyers only 'advise', and they never get the blame when a writ does land on the Editor's desk. I am still puzzled as to why newspapers bother with them.

Anyway this particular lawyer was called Tom Crone and, by a strange twist of fate, we knew each other fleetingly during our teenage years. I remembered him vividly because we had a silly adolescent run-in outside a particularly noisy party in Raynes Park. To this day he says he doesn't remember the incident, but then you know what lawyers are like . . . Despite all this Tom and I were on good terms. He was probably the finest news-paper lawyer I ever came across because he was on the same social level as us journalists. He understood exactly how we operated and always took that into account. Most lawyers simply didn't have a clue . . .

Bob handed the phone over to Tom.

'Hello, Wensley. Did you tape record any of your phone conversations?'

'Well, no, actually.' For the first time I felt slightly nervous. 'The circumstances just weren't right for it. But I had witnesses throughout.'

I couldn't actually remember if that was the case, but I knew that was the answer they were looking for. Fleet Street is all about giving people what they want. That's why tabloids sell so well and how reporters like me make a living.

Bob then came back on the line: 'Don't worry, Wensley.

We're just running through a few things here. Speak to you later.'

But I was worried, and I knew Bob Edwards was as well.

Back to my beloved screwdriver. This time I manage four turns before, you've guessed it, the phone rang again.

'Hello, Bob here. Sorry to trouble you again.' Doesn't mean a word of it as usual. 'But the lawyer forgot to ask you one important question.'

Over to Tom Crone. 'Wensley, do you think that this free-lancer who supplied the story made it all up?'

If he did it seemed a bit late to worry about it now. What a thought. The Man Mountain of Chippenham might have con-jured the whole thing up. He could so easily have got a friend to act out the role of the grey policeman. That social club scene could easily have been arranged. Then again, I was the only person who'd actually been there, and while my experiences might not have sounded particularly impressive in a court of law, there was no doubt in my mind that Mountain was straight.

'It's all absolutely true. This guy has all the right connections. I have no doubt whatsoever that he was telling the truth.' I realised I was beginning to sound like a tape recorder.

Back to Bob the Editor. 'OK, Wensley. I just wanted to hear it from you.'

Hear it from me? I must have repeated it at least a dozen times. It was a game of pass the buck, and I knew someone was going to end up in a heap of trouble when the music stopped. But what could I do other than play on. So I returned to my patient screwdriver.

With the first baton successfully screwed to the wall, I was beginning to relax. Then the dreaded machine summoned me once more. I had enjoyed at least three minutes of silence.

'Hello, Wensley. Bob here.'

This was getting boring. I had to get these shelves up or else I'd be in big trouble at home. The threat of a writ from Prince Charles didn't concern me half so much as my lamentable progress with the shelves. What could I do to stop Bob Edwards from ruining my day off? One call at home from the Editor is a privilege, but four is a plain nuisance. I had to think of something – and quick. Then I remembered a trick I'd seen played by Hollywood star James Garner on the 'Rockford Files' late one night.

'Hello, Bob. Bob? Can you hear me?'

'Yes, Wensley. What's wrong?'

Severe crackling on the phone line followed – this being caused by me tapping the buttons on the telephone.

'Did you hear that Bob?' More tapping and crackling.

'Yes, Wensley. It's a very bad line. Sounds like interference.'

He was nibbling at the bait so I moved in for the kill.

'I don't think it is interference, Bob.'

'What do you mean Wensley?'

'Gremlins, Bob. Gremlins.'

'I think I know what you mean.'

'Bob, it would be better if we continued this conversation in person. Face to face.'

'Absolutely, Wensley. See you in the office at ten tomorrow.'

End of phone pestering from Editor.

The inference was that Buckingham Palace had authorised a phone tap to find out who was the source of our world exclusive. I leave you to make up your own mind as to whether that was likely.

The next day, Tuesday, was my first in the office since the Royal Train Story (or scandal, depending on what paper you read) had broken. All the daily tabloids had decided, in their traditionally bloodthirsty way, that this was a running story – which meant they were likely to carry articles about it all week. But unlike most big stories which are followed up by the dailies, it was the denial rather than the story itself that dominated the headlines. PALACE FURY OVER ROYAL TRAIN STORY was the sort of thing being published. The atmosphere in the office was tense to say the least. I walked in, sat at my desk, opened my mail and PJ didn't even acknowledge my presence. What a difference from a week earlier.

As I sat there nervously twiddling with my typewriter and

trying to look busy, many worried thoughts went through my mind. Maybe Bob Edwards had told PJ to sack me? Perhaps I was going to have to submit to a lie detector test? Maybe Man Mountain had rung up the Editor and told him he made it all up in a fit of depression. I couldn't stand it any longer. I had to talk to PJ. So I wandered over to the news desk to see if I could catch his eye.

He looked up. I looked down. Then I heard his voice. 'Cheer up, mate. You haven't been summoned to the Tower yet!'

Then it dawned on me why he hadn't leapt on me the moment I walked into the office. Like all of us, he had his priorities firmly in the right order. PJ was doing his expenses. If I'd asked him why he was doing them in such a period of crisis no doubt he would have cheerfully replied: 'Got to get 'em in before we all get the boot, mate.' There I was, terrified that my journalistic career might be at an end, when in fact I was just the innocent victim of an executive's urge to get his exes done on time.

PJ looked up from his calculator and offered up his first thought of the day on the Royal Train 'problem' (it had developed rapidly from story to problem in *Sunday Mirror* terms).

'I think you'll be seeing a lot more of Chippenham over the next few weeks, mate.'

That was indeed bad news. Not only did I hate long-running stories, as you know, but I knew instinctively this was going to mean more and more trouble. Before I could even pass comment, PJ leapt up from his desk and shot off in the direction of the Editor's office. I didn't need three guesses to work out what he was going to discuss with him.

On his return, PJ looked flustered. He told me that Buckingham Palace's press chief Michael Shea was insisting the *Sunday Mirror* publish a retraction. That would make us the laughing stock of Fleet Street. Besides that, we stood by our story.

The Palace did concede that the Prince had stayed aboard his train on the nights in question. It was a mere morsel of a concession, but it seemed oddly reassuring to PJ and me. All the same, we were up to our necks and the tide of opprobrium was rising.

'There's only one thing we can do,' said PJ. 'We'll have to start the whole story all over again. We are going to prove every single aspect of it, in triplicate if necessary. Right. Off you go to Chippenham. Now.'

So it was that I set off to Wiltshire once more on this weird assignment to prove a story that had already been written and published in my paper.

With me this time I took a new assistant called Nick Ferrari. He came from a family steeped in tabloid newspaper tradition – he knew how to play the game.

The first couple of days in the Chippenham area were odd to say the least. The fact that we were trying to stand up an old story made motivation difficult. But as PJ pointed out, 'This one's more important than any splash. This is a matter of survival.'

We constantly seemed to be chasing shadows or leads that didn't stand up. Every few hours, Nick Ferrari and I would meet up with Man Mountain to exchange snippets of info. But all to no avail. As the week passed by, we became more and more twitchy and Man Mountain was veering towards paranoia. By Thursday, he was insisting I ring the phone twice before he would answer and he even introduced a silly Secret Squirrel type code for ringing the front door bell. To make matters even worse, I had started to believe my own phone-tap con on Bob Edwards. Since PJ and Man Mountain were already convinced I was right about the tap, the result was a series of absurdly coded telephone conversations like: 'Everything A OK down at CRS [Chippenham Railway Siding]. Spoken to local contact who firmed up car info.' My initial feeling that Inspector Clouseau would have fitted in perfectly with this business was proving more than a little prophetic.

The whole affair was getting out of hand. It was bloody ridiculous. All we'd done was brand Prince Charles a bit of a

Romeo. I would have thought his reputation needed that sort of boost in the early 1980s . . .

Now the whole pack of daily paper newshounds was on our trail and baying for blood. They were out in full force in the Wiltshire area, trying their damnedest to prove the Royal Train story was a pack of lies. The newspaper most active in this department was the *Daily Mail*, which had teams of hacks turning over every stone and sifting every grain of information. I later discovered the reason for this obsessional (even by Fleet Street standards) behaviour. It turned out that the *Mail* had an old score to settle with the *Sunday Mirror*. Some years previously, the *Sunday Mirror* had launched a scathing public attack on the *Mail* after they published a so-called exposé of Lord Ryder and a British Leyland slush fund. It then turned out the *Mail* had been elaborately hoaxed by a conman. And in the finest dog eat dog tradition, the *Sunday Mirror* blasted out an editorial condemning the whole story as a disgrace. Now it was the *Mail* that was on the attack and I can tell you (having worked there) they go in hard. Since the paper appeals to women and estate agents, people assume it is far more respectable than the *Sun* or *Star*. That's nonsense in my opinion, though it has to be said that the *Mail* is a brilliantly edited paper that is always an entertaining read.

If all the other tabloids send one reporter out to doorstep a love-tangled pop star, then the *Mail* will send three. Associated Newspapers (the *Mail*'s owners) have always made sure they get exactly what they want. If Sir David or any of his team of tough Assistant Editors are interested in a particular story, then it gets covered in triplicate – simple as that. The *Mail*'s newsroom at that time was manned by herds of young reporters keen as mustard to deliver the goods. The result was that once a team of *Mail* rookies was out on a story, there was little anyone could do to contain them. The older hands just sat back and watched, but it has to be said that they did often score where others failed – as poor old Man Mountain discovered to his cost towards the end of that trouble-torn week. PJ had sensibly put Mountain on a weekly retainer from the moment the shit began hitting the fan – it was his way of ensuring that he did as he was told. We had warned Mountain not to talk to anyone – 'not even the fucking milkman,' I told him. But basically Mountain was a lonely soul, and when he found an instant new friend from the *Mail* standing on his doorstep, he just couldn't resist. It nearly proved the downfall of all of us.

Once inside Man Mountain's house, the eager young *Mail* scribe moved in for the kill. By the time he left Number 23 Frogmore, severe doubts had been cast on the story – thanks to Mountain's own concession that the information might not all have been completely accurate. The *Mail* also discovered that the kind old *Sunday Mirror* was paying Mountain a 'little something' to keep him going while the heat was on.

When the artful young hack's words landed on the desk of Sir David English he must have been rubbing his hands in glee. Next day the *Mail* ran a leader demanding that the *Sunday Mirror* be punished for its treasonable story on Prince Charles. Touché. Another dog bites the dust. Also on the attack in the same paper was gossip columnist Nigel Dempster. He cheekily challenged Bob Edwards to a wager of £10,000 that he couldn't prove the story was true. He kept on trashing the story in his column until I began to feel thoroughly pissed off with him. It will therefore come as no surprise that some years later I tried to run him over when he was out jogging with his pet poodle (don't sue Nige, it might have been a Yorkshire terrier) near his South Kensington home. Since he was dressed in a very tasteful purple tracksuit, you would have thought I could hardly miss him. He was no doubt totally unaware that I was thinking about squashing him, and anyway, I missed. The truth is, I lost my bottle at the last moment.

Everyone seemed to be buckling under the pressure except me. I was the lucky one wandering around in huge circles of Wiltshire countryside. It was now Friday afternoon (six days after publication). I checked in by phone from the Chippenham district. The one thing I had achieved during my travels was finding a comfortable, warm, clean phone box that no one else seemed to know about. All I could provide PJ with was a lot of false hope. News Editors always expect a development on every phone call from a reporter out on the road. Normally, I would store up information and gradually release one or two facts at a time spread across at least four check-in calls every day. It usually had the desired effect of making PJ believe I was working my arse off the whole time – which of course I wasn't. One reason why I'd brought along Nick Ferrari was that he was a keen participator in exactly the same game. Often I would check in to PJ within minutes of Nick and pretending I hadn't seen him for hours. In fact we were together, but PJ liked to think that if we were working separately we would achieve much more. But reporters love working in pairs because they can cover for each other much more easily.

The problem with this particular situation was that since we were trying to prove a story that had already been published, I was beginning to run out of non-facts to throw at PJ. As it happened he wasn't interested in what I was up to. He wanted to let me know what was happening his end.

PJ told me that Bob Edwards was planning to publish a letter of denial from the Palace. I was astounded. We would all end up looking complete fools.

'Hang on a minute. Let me finish,' said PJ. He went on to tell me that the Editor was going to publish the *Sunday Mirror*'s own words insisting the story *was* true alongside this Palace waffle. It seemed an effective if somewhat roundabout way of keeping everyone happy. The idea was that the whole story would be dead and buried once and for all after we published the piece on Sunday.

Unfortunately it didn't work out that way. The Royal Train was going to carry on running and running. Journalists from papers and television stations around the world were taking even more interest in this saga, and were even starting to investigate me. Now if there's one thing that makes a reporter nervous it is when other journalists start sticking their nose into your affairs. I found myself briefing Clare, my wife, on how to avoid talking to reporters, who had already started ringing up and calling at my house. It was all so ironic. Here was I telling my family how to make sure some keen young scribe like myself didn't stitch us up. An American TV network wanted me to appear on screen, and for a moment I was tempted. Someone might see me, be impressed and offer me a job. It was a silly thought, but I wasn't exactly suffering from job security at the time. PJ vetoed the idea instantly. 'Don't be silly,' he told me. 'These people might make you look an idiot. Steer clear of them.' It was yet another irony in a long list of them.

While all this was going on, Man Mountain was definitely beginning to crack up. He kept ringing me or PJ to say he wasn't that confident about the grey policeman. It was the last thing we wanted to hear. Thereafter, one unfortunate hack was assigned sentry duty outside the Mountain's home. It wasn't a pleasant tour of duty, as Jimbo was attacking anything that moved at that time. But we all knew we had to tread very carefully with Man Mountain. Rival reporters were still snooping around Chippenham, anxious to offer him a fortune in exchange for a confession that he made the whole thing up.

Publication of the Palace denial and the *Sunday Mirror*'s defence came and went but still the fuss would not die down. Man Mountain was getting more and more agitated, and I told PJ I was worried he might finish off all our careers. In a desperate bid to calm Mountain down, PJ decided he'd have to make a flying visit to Number 23 Frogmore. By the time we arrived chez Mountain, I'd briefed PJ thoroughly and he knew exactly what to expect. On stepping through the front door he said politely: 'Nice place you got here, mate.' There followed an outstanding performance, even by PJ's high standards. He might not have been on the road for five years, but PJ knew how to switch on the charm, and we needed Mountain on our side. He patted Jimbo. He knocked back Mountain's cuppa as if he was drinking the finest Indian in the Fountain Restaurant at Fortnum & Mason. He was in his element – the truth is, PJ had me under his spell as well. But our host was clearly in a bad way. He said he'd had enough and he looked to me as if he was on the verge of a nervous breakdown. PJ reassured him brilliantly, showing flashes of a bedside manner that would put most GPs to shame.

An hour later we said our farewells. I dropped PJ at Chippenham Railway Station and set once more to combing the Wiltshire countryside for meaningless clues that might help me prove what was by now a positively geriatric story. Six weeks, seventy check-in phone calls and twelve return journeys down the M4 later we were finally pulled off the story.

The dust had finally settled. A complaint to the Press Council made by a Mr Angry of Wimbledon was withdrawn – in fact throughout his career PJ never had a complaint against him upheld by the Press Council, an enviable record for a tabloid News Editor. None of us were sacked. The Palace never sued us for libel and I was just desperate to work on a story that had nothing to do with trains or the royal family.

TWO
Welcome to Fleet Street

It was a crisp, clear sunny day in January and I was feeling distinctly bored. I hadn't been on a good rip-roaring yarn for quite a few weeks, and I couldn't see any great stories on the horizon either. Nor was I looking forward to struggling through the South London traffic to spend a whole Wednesday 'creating' a convincing set of expenses to cover the previous week of inactivity.

As I lay in bed surrounded by my three baby children – who'd been kicking me in the groin for most of the night – I seriously considered not bothering to go in to work. I must be getting old, I thought to myself, at the age of twenty-four.

Then, without prior warning, a set of newspapers landed a direct hit on my weary face. My darling wife had grabbed them from the doorstep and hurled them in my direction – so thoughtful. One of the biggest annoyances about being married to a journalist is the incredible number of newspapers and magazines that end up scattered round the house. On a normal day I would have all the tabloids plus at least two so-called 'heavies' delivered to my home. So it was hardly surprising that the weight of these papers landing on my face snapped me out of my lethargy. I kept to the same reading routine every morning. I would start with *The Sun*, move to the *Daily Mail* and then switch to the *Daily Mirror*. By the time I had read all three, I reckoned to have taken in ninety per cent of tabloid world news for the day.

On this particular morning I went through my favoured routine, and by the time I'd got half way through the *Mirror* was feeling distinctly depressed again. Quite simply, there wasn't one good story to follow up for the *Sunday Mirror*. What on earth was I going to do all week? I knew that my beloved news editor P.J. Wilson was obsessed by the need to follow up big stories in the daily papers, but there was nothing to chase. Another strain-free week in Holborn Circus trying to stand up useless tip-offs from desperate freelancers. What a drag.

To make matters worse, as I lay in bed I felt a pool of water forming under my thigh. No, pool is the wrong word. It was a gushing torrent, and my leg felt sticky. I looked under the sheets and noticed that my bottomless two-year-old had decided to abandon his potty training in favour of a far simpler method. It was at that unfortunate point that I turned to the Peter McKay diary page near the centre of the *Daily Mirror*. My attention was caught by a very strange lead article on an actor going off on holiday to the Caribbean with a sixteen-year-old girl. I read on and discovered they had only departed the day before. The actor was Oliver Reed.

Now it just happened that I lived in Reed's old stomping ground of Wimbledon and I vaguely knew his son Mark. At nineteen he was somewhat older than his old man's travelling companion. That in itself seemed a good line to pursue. The extraordinary thing about the article in question was that it didn't even name the young girl, and it also lacked details of exactly where the two had gone. But then it was only a diary story, and they tend not to be very detailed. But this was what astonished me most. Why had the *Daily Mirror* failed to recognise the potential of the story their diarist had written and hidden it in the column, rather than developing it into a fully-blown news story – as I fully intended to do myself?

A combination of my baby son's wee and my interest in this obvious scoop sparked me into action and I grabbed the phone and rang PJ at home. Damn. He'd already left for the office. Not surprising, I guess, since he lived in deepest Kent and faced a two-hour journey each way into work. Suddenly I felt really desperate to get into work. Having woken in an apathetic state which rapidly turned to damp depression, I had now gone full circle and felt absurdly optimistic and full of vim.

Almost immediately the curse of all Fleet Street operators set in – paranoia. What if someone else had read the article in question? After all, three million people did read the *Mirror* every day. I suppose it was reasonable to expect the odd journalist to be amongst them. More worrying still, perhaps one of my rivals on the *Sunday Mirror* was going through exactly the same thought process as myself. There was only one thing for it. I would have to get into the office at least half-an-hour early and wait for PJ to emerge from the lift so I could nab the story first. I bathed and dressed at high speed and refused all offers of breakfast. As I fought my way through the screaming babies and screaming wife towards the front door my only thoughts were on Oliver Reed and a sumptuous Caribbean location. I had to get there – I had to be the one to crack it.

Driving through the thick, slow South London traffic, I twisted and turned into every short-cut I knew in a crazed attempt to get to that office before anyone else. Forty-five minutes later I drove at breakneck speed down the '5 mph Max' ramp into the *Mirror*'s underground car park, ignoring the cursing of the attendant and various other unfortunates who got in my way. Just a few minutes later I emerged from the lift at the fifth floor and ran into the open plan office that doubled as newsroom and rubbish tip for the *Sunday Mirror*.

Not a soul was in. I had missed breakfast, nearly killed myself on the streets of South London, and even ignored the Chairman when he'd tried to stop for a chat – all to make sure I got in with the story first. And no one was fucking well in! Rather than drown in my own disappointment, I decided to take the Ollie Reed story as far as I could on the phone while waiting for PJ to appear. I started ringing round all my Wimbledon friends in an effort to locate Reed's minder who, according to the *Daily Mirror* piece, had accompanied the two on their sojourn in the sun.

It was during one of these calls that PJ merrily strolled in to the newsroom looking, as he always did, as if he hadn't a care in the world. 'Morning, Wense,' he yelled across to me, failing to spot the telephone receiver glued to my right ear. I nodded and at the same time established that the contact I was talking to didn't have a clue where Reed's minder had gone. I slammed down the phone and made for PJ's desk. But at that precise moment he picked up the phone and dialled out. My heart sank. I had to tell him, and now. So I walked round to the area right next to his chaotic desk and stood deliberately close by, hoping he would feel so inhibited by my presence that he'd stop talking on the phone and give me my story. Unfortunately my ploy failed completely. PJ could be a pretty thick-skinned person at times – and this was one of them. After ten minutes of shuffling round his desk, I turned to walk away, completely deflated by my failure to talk to him. Then I heard the welcome clunk of the receiver hitting the cradle and I turned back to have my say.

'PJ, look at this,' I said, thrusting the McKay column under his nose.

He looked blankly at it. Obviously he hadn't even noticed it whilst reading the papers on the 7.40 from Faversham. The silence was killing me so I committed a sin that tabloid journalists regularly manage. I took a flyer. By that I mean I pretended I was already in possession of new information about the story that would guarantee I would be assigned it.

'I know where they're staying in the Caribbean and I've got the home address of the son and minder. With any luck I'll soon have the details on the girl as well,' I lied blatantly.

PJ looked ecstatic. He'd obviously been feeling the same way about that morning's papers as I had, and wondering where he'd find a hot story to put on the schedule for the first editorial conference of the week later that day. He was more than happy to clutch at the odd straw and, let's face it, that was absolutely all I had to offer at that stage.

'Fantastic, mate. Get stuck in to it. You'll be on your way to the West Indies at this rate!' he said, not meaning a word of it.

I was like a bull in a china shop. I had to have this story at any cost. Within seconds of leaving PJ's side I was hitting the phones in a desperate search for all the information I'd told him I already had. It's funny how things go. If you really believe you're going to achieve something, nine times out of ten you do. Especially if you put the extra pressure of a few lies to live up to on yourself. That is precisely what happened that morning. I was doggedly determined to take PJ up on his promise of a glamorous trip to the Caribbean. Soon I had the name of the street in Wimbledon where Reed's minder lived, I had Mark Reed's phone number and address, and I had established that the girl lived near Ollie's country seat in Ockley, Surrey.

By lunchtime I was knocking on doors in a shabby road in downtown Wimbledon, speaking to neighbours of the minder. One old dear happily volunteered the information that he was in Barbados for two weeks with 'Mr Reed, the famous film star'. I was beginning to get somewhere. Next came Mark Reed. He was the spitting image of his old man – tall and dark, with those piercing blue eyes that made Reed one of the best looking actors of his day. The problem with Mark was that he wasn't a thespian he was a salesman, and he lived, to a certain degree, in the shadow of his father.

He wasn't at home when I called round, but when I telephoned half-way through the afternoon Mark answered the phone and couldn't resist filling me in on the details of his Dad's holiday plans. Mark only knew the girl's first name, but what he did do was give me the name of the villa on Barbados where they were all staying. I honestly don't think that he actually realised why I was asking until after I'd put the phone down.

By this time, the only thing on my mind was the weather in Barbados at that time of year. Everyone kept telling me January was the ideal month, not too hot but not too rainy either. It all sounded perfect to me, but before my beach'n'cocktails dreams came true I had to take a slightly shorter and less agreeable trip to Ockley, in Surrey, to carry on my research into the girl's family.

Ockley is a strange place. It's neither real countryside nor real suburbia – and certainly lacks the charm of a village a long way from London. My first objective was to find Ollie Reed's house near the village and work outwards from there. It wasn't difficult to track down. As I drove along what seemed like a quiet country lane I couldn't help but notice a life-size plastic rhino standing by the gates of an impressive looking country house. I had arrived at the court of jester Reed.

The house was completely dead – not surprising, really, when you consider that its master was six thousand miles away lapping up the Barbados sun. But by finding the house, I could establish a most important bit of background info – where the nearest pub was. I didn't need to be Einstein to know that any local hostelries would know all about hard-drinking Oliver Reed.

It was about seven in the evening when I walked into Reed's local. It was a Wednesday and I knew the only flight to the West Indies that would get me there in time to complete the story and file for the first Sunday edition was at nine-thirty the next morning. It was the ultimate incentive.

In the pub I approached the locals tactfully – no mention of being a newspaperman. That would be the worst move of all. I said I was a friend of Reed's and couldn't understand why he wasn't in because I had an important appointment with him.

'Oh, he's gone off on holiday,' said the landlord. How did the landlord know you might ask. It turned out Reed had hosted a massive farewell party at the pub the night before his departure. He must be one of the few people in the world who has a farewell party just before he goes on a two-week holiday!

Soon I had established all the facts I needed. The name of the girl, where she went to school, and – most important of all – where she lived. As it happened it was opposite the pub. My luck was in and I was sure I was on my way to Barbados.

A hard knock on a thick wooden door belonging to a rather twee little house was my next move. It was the home of Josephine Burge – Ollie Reed's Barbados companion. A young man answered and told me his sister was away in the West Indies without even bothering to ask me who I was. It is extraordinary how many people will tell you all sorts of secrets before even making that simple request.

Not surprisingly my reply, when he did finally ask, didn't go down too well and – not for the first or last time in my career –

the door was firmly closed in my face. But I didn't care. I already had enough. I was cock-a-hoop.

There was now just one small obstacle between me and the beach – P.J. Wilson. When it came to crunch time, PJ had to be certain it was worth sending me, and that meant a sixth degree interrogation. Finding a phone box in a place like Ockley shouldn't really have proved too difficult, you would have thought . . . wouldn't you? It took me over an hour of cruising round vandalised phone boxes before I managed to get through to PJ, by now back at his own country home in Kent.

'I've got it all, PJ,' I exclaimed.

'Great, mate,' he replied hesitantly. I knew he was considering backtracking on the Barbados carrot that had been dangled before me so enticingly just a few hours earlier. Immediately I began bombarding him with the facts I had established.

By the end of the conversation he asked me, typically, 'Are you sure, Wense?'

I took a gulp and assured him: 'I have no doubt that Reed, the minder and the girl are in Barbados now. You've got to let me go there.'

'What time's the flight in the morning?'

'It leaves at nine-thirty. There's not another one till Friday.'

'Oh, right . . . ' PJ sounded heartbroken that I was so far ahead of the game. Maybe he was hoping that I wouldn't know the flight times and that would mean a further delay. No chance. I was a Fleet Street journalist for Christ's sake!

A short silence followed. I didn't know what to say so I just held my breath.

'Off you go then, mate. Ring me from the airport.'

I couldn't believe my ears. He'd given the trip the go ahead. I laughed out loud to myself as I walked back to the car. I was delirious.

Little did I know what lay in store for me.

I got home at about eleven that night. The whole family were asleep so I crept into bed and just lay there, veering from joy to dread and back again as I thought about the adventure I was about to embark on. It was slowly dawning on me that I had committed myself to success on a story that would cost the *Sunday Mirror* thousands of pounds in air fares and expenses alone. In reality I still had a long way to go before I had the complete tale. Barbados, in fact. If this didn't turn out to be one of my best stories, I'd need my best excuses when I got back.

Next morning I was up at the crack of dawn. As usual the babies were sprawled across the entire bed, having all insisted on sleeping with us. I packed my ludicrously small overnight bag without once thinking about the hot climate I was about to travel to. But the weather in Barbados had long since left my thoughts. I was panicking. I was terrified. Maybe the whole story was going to be a massive cock-up. Maybe when I got there I'd discover that Reed *et al* had decided they couldn't take the heat and taken the first flight back to good old England.

It was a pointless line of thought, but PJ's last words to me kept ringing in my ears: 'Are you sure they are there, mate? I'd hate you to go all that way and find they're not around.'

I drove to Heathrow Airport in a sort of daze. Why the hell had I pursued the story in the first place? At the check-in I was as nervous as an unaccompanied minor. I broke out in a hot sweat, and as the perspiration streamed off my face the check-in lady from British West Indian Airways looked terribly concerned. 'Are you OK, sir?' she asked with a delightful West Indian smile. 'Fine,' I said. It didn't exactly describe my feelings, but what else could I say?

Then came the big moment. The check-in phone call to P.J. Wilson. Would he tell me to abandon the trip? I hoped so. I was by now utterly paranoid. I'd decided a trip to Barbados was the very worst thing one could experience in life. Or maybe the pessimist inside me kept thinking that way so I wouldn't be too disappointed if PJ called the trip off. I was in such a stew I didn't know what I was feeling. As it happened, PJ didn't have a great deal to say to me except: 'Get on the plane, mate. You lucky bastard.'

I have omitted to mention so far that I am terrified of flying. I'd even forgotten this myself – until I boarded the plane and felt my stomach lurch. It turned an entirely civilised flight with BWIA into a second nightmare that competed violently in my head with my fears and doubts about the story I was chasing. When the ropey old Tristar finally touched down at Bridgetown Airport, I was one hell of a relieved man, I can tell you. On one count, anyway . . .

In any other business of an international nature, a colleague or contact would normally be at the airport to greet you on arrival in a strange and foreign land. Not so in the highly organised world of tabloid newspapers, I am afraid. For half an hour I wandered around aimlessly looking for a car hire office. It was Thursday afternoon local time and I couldn't afford to wait till the morning to start work. To be honest, in the back of my mind was the thought that if the story proved to be a red herring I could take my red face on the flight back to London the next day and no one but PJ would know I'd had anything to do with this disaster.

Eventually I managed to hire a beaten up old Datsun and, with my accommodation details scribbled on a scrap of paper, I set off up country to the exquisitely named Coconut Grove Hotel. Funnily enough, it was not a difficult place to find and I checked in at high speed, anxious to sling my stuff in my room and zoom round to the villa where the Reed ensemble were gathered.

My luck still seemed to be holding. The hotel manageress knew exactly where the villa was – just half a mile up the road. Within minutes of checking in, I was struggling up the west coast of this famous island in search of a film star with a reputation for thumping people, his minder – no doubt a hard nut too – and a sixteen-year-old girl. I should have known better!

The villa was surrounded by a ten-foot-high wall, and locked gates blocked the entrance to the driveway. But through the wrought iron I could see Reed in the garden, so I hailed him brightly.

'Hello, Mr Reed, could I have a quick word?'

He ignored me. Nothing unusual in that – except that I was standing in a roadway in Barbados and he didn't even know what I wanted. But nothing was going to budge our Ollie. He steadfastly refused to acknowledge my existence. I felt deflated. Then another man approached me from a side entrance to the huge villa. He looked well hard, and I didn't need three guesses to work out that he was the minder. 'I don't know what you want, but why don't you fuck off,' explained the minder gently.

It dawned on me that someone in England – probably the son Mark – had tipped them off that the press were in hot pursuit. But in case I was wrong I wasn't going to say anything about being a journalist just yet.

'You work for the *Mirror*, don't you?'

I tried to look flabbergasted.

'Come on, mate. We knew you were on your way.'

Suddenly I felt as if I was the one being exposed. My cover was blown and I'd only been on the island for about an hour.

'Just fuck off out of here and don't come back.'

'But you don't even know why I am here,' I protested lamely.

It was no good, I was on a hiding to nothing and I knew it. I retreated to the relative safety of my hotel.

I was feeling down but certainly not out when I flopped onto my bed, exhausted from the jet-lag and the disappointment of not scoring a direct hit on my first attempt.

Then I suddenly remembered that I had the phone number of the villa and I decided to give it a call. The minder answered and he seemed in a much better mood for some odd reason. Maybe Ollie wasn't in the room so he didn't have to act tough. Anyway, he seemed vaguely willing to have a conversation with me.

'I'm sorry I had to give you a bollocking, but Ollie's like a raging bull at the moment. He's got the flu and he's feeling very protective towards Josephine. He feels a responsibility to look after her and he doesn't want to upset her mum back in England since they are neighbours.'

I couldn't believe what I was hearing. It was most definitely a very encouraging step. The minder just seemed happy to be talking to an English voice. You know what it's like when you've been stuck in a foreign country for days.

Anyway, I decided it was time to move in for the kill, so I asked the minder casually: 'Why don't you come down here to the Coconut Grove and have a drink? It's the least I can do in the circumstances.'

'I might very well do that. I feel right cooped up being here all day and night, and I'm desperate for a bar and a cold beer,' said the minder.

We bade our goodbyes and I lay down on the bed and wondered whether he would really turn up.

About an hour and a half later the phone in my room rang. No, it wasn't the minder. I was disappointed. Instead it was Charles, a local photographer commissioned by my office in London to accompany me round the island. Basically they were too sharp to send a snapper with me from London on such a long-shot assignment, so they hired some cheap labour instead. Charles was in reception waiting for me, so I strolled past the pool and the obligatory palm trees through to the lobby of the hotel to meet my brand new colleague.

Just as I had shaken his hand, a familiar sight approached me from the main entrance to the lobby. It was Minder, all six feet square of him, and he looked really pleased to be at the hotel. But it was the person with him who left me open-mouthed. She looked about sixteen, slight with elfin features.

'This is Josephine, mate,' said Minder, failing like the rest of the world to remember what my name was.

She looked shyly at me and shook my hand, but said nothing apart from, 'Hello.'

I couldn't believe my luck. Just a few hours earlier I couldn't even get through the gates to their villa but now here was Josephine coming into my hotel for a drink, and with *me*. It was bizarre to say the very least.

Meanwhile, sweet old Charles the photographer looked on in amazement. He had never even heard of Ollie Reed, and must have wondered what on earth these two had to do with his assignment.

So we all sat at the bar and I ordered a round of rum punches – what else do you expect in Barbados? I ignored Minder's plea for a cold beer, despite our earlier telephone conversation. Chatting was not easy to start with. I deliberately avoided all mention of Mr Reed and talked about the joys of living in the countryside instead. It was hardly a subject I know much about as I was born and bred in London, but they weren't to know that. The rum punches were soon going down at a tremendous rate but still I hadn't dared bring up the subject at hand. In fact, instead of us all relaxing and having a laugh, the going was getting stickier by the minute.

Then, without warning, Josephine turned towards me and said, as cool as a cucumber: 'He's a fantastic bloke and I don't care what you write about us.'

Minder nearly dropped his drink. No doubt Reed had briefed them both not to get pissed and start talking about anything vaguely relevant and here she was volunteering info.

I took an enormous risk and said to her: 'Look, we're not here to talk about all that. We're just here to have a good drink and nothing else.'

Minder looked relieved. What he didn't realise was that I had decided the best way to get the maximum out of her was to win her trust. That's why I had changed the subject so fast. Besides, neither of them was yet pissed enough to spill the beans completely!

It worked a treat. Josephine looked thankfully at me, and we got stuck into another four or five rounds of rum punch. Only after that did I steer the conversation gently in the desired direction. This time, Josephine really opened up. As they say in Fleet Street, she told the lot.

At this delicate stage you might be wondering why Minder hadn't stepped in to protect innocent young Josephine. The answer was quite simple, really. The rum punches had some-how got the better of him and he had zonked out on a sofa. As he snored away like a contented baby, I continued to pump

Josephine in the nicest possible way. As the evening progressed I began to realise that Josephine was really quite mature for her years. In fact she was a rather motherly type – the perfect companion for the enfant terrible.

Charles, my friendly native snapper, still couldn't believe his eyes. This obviously wasn't the way journalists on the *Barbados Times* behaved. But to his credit, he never once complained. Instead, he politely refused every single one of my offers to buy him one of those lethal concoctions.

Drunk I may have been, but I still retained my professional nous, as Charles was about to find out. I knew the only thing missing from my great coup was the man himself, Mr Oliver Reed, and I knew I had to get to him. However, I hadn't forgotten what Minder had told me earlier, that Reed was in a foul mood because he had caught a bout of flu. How, you may ask, can someone catch flu in ninety degrees of sunshine? It seems that Mr Reed and Josephine had stopped off in Vermont, USA, for a spot of skiing before arriving in the Caribbean. Not surprisingly, the sudden change in temperature had the unde-sired effect on the normally robust Mr Reed. The result was what Minder pleasantly described as 'a bear with a fucking sore head'. And he even warned me: 'He'll fucking kill you if you go anywhere near the villa again.'

With that dire warning still ringing in my ears, I took a mighty gulp of my rum punch and decided there was only one thing for it – I would have to launch an Entebbe-style raid on the villa in question. God alone knows how I came to this foolhardy conclusion. I guess that although I hadn't completely taken leave of my senses I must have been in possession of several gallons of Dutch courage. Snorting appreciatively at the dregs of my punch, I told myself that nothing and no one was going to stop me seeing Mr Oliver Reed that evening.

But I still had to devise a way of slipping out of the hotel bar with Charles unnoticed by Josephine. Not an easy task in the circumstances. A mixture of pure good fortune and utter greed brought on by the vast amounts of alcohol I had consumed resulted in a plan that to my befuddled brain seemed little short of Napoleonic.

'God, I am fucking starving,' I shouted towards Charles and Josephine (Minder was still snoozing on the sofa). 'Can we get some dinner here?' I asked the bartender. The answer was no, as I very well knew it would be. It was ten-thirty, and they'd stopped serving dinner at least an hour earlier.

'Where can we grab some food, Charles?' I asked with a definite slur.

'There are some chicken bars near here. We could go to one of them,' came my comrade's answer.

One of the many strange things about Barbados is the vast number of Kentucky Fried Chicken takeaways that litter the roadside. With a speed limit of twenty-five mph throughout the island, you can hardly fail to notice them.

Anyway, at this point I turned to Josephine and Minder, who was just struggling to awaken from his slumber, and said 'I'm just popping out for some takeaway grub. I'll be back in five minutes.' They nodded in approval and I made sure Minder bought another round of rum punches to convince them I would be back as soon as I said.

As soon as I had squeezed into the passenger seat of Charles' tiny Mini, I turned to the increasingly bemused snapper and said: 'Forget the chicken, mate. We're off to Reed's villa.'

Now Charles was beginning to look positively scared, but he wasn't about to back out now and we set off with a prolonged rattle and a blast of exhaust. It was great to see that the relationship between reporters and photographers had not declined to the point it had in London, where snappers would often refuse to go on certain of the more intrepid assignments. Clearly Charles knew I was in charge, though he probably wished I wasn't. Within two or three minutes we were approaching the villa. We were in luck – the gates were open. Tut, tut. Minder and Josephine had failed to shut them on their way to meet me. I barked at Charles to drive in and up the two-hundred-yard private driveway that led to the villa itself. Charles was looking even more unrelaxed but I was way past caring. The combination of Dutch courage and pure excitement was driving me on relentlessly.

On getting out of the Mini, I noticed all the doors and windows were wide open so I took that as a welcoming gesture on the part of the Reed household and ran – well, weaved is probably more like it – up the steps to the porch. Inside a TV was blaring and a half-empty glass was sitting on a table. I knew my prey was here so, being a well-mannered sort of chap, I knocked on the door. There was no reply so I knocked again and called out, 'Mr Reed. Mr Reed? Are you in?' It's an incongruous habit of many reporters to call their victims 'Mister'. It's almost as if we need to lure our subjects into a false sense of security before launching our front-page splashes. Anyway, calling Reed Mister didn't work particularly well on this occasion because he still wasn't answering. I began to get frustrated. I knew he was in the villa and I knew I had to see him.

'Bugger this,' I thought to myself. 'He's in here and I'm going to find him.' I was about to take a huge risk with a man who was renowned for his ability to punch. But, as Mr Reed himself would no doubt agree, drink does that to you. Here goes . . .

I decided there and then to search the whole house from top to bottom. Charles, who wasn't privy to my innermost thoughts, had managed to read my mind – more than I was capable of, quite frankly – and he stepped back into his Mini and waited while I carried out the raid. I realised there was no way a local coloured photographer would want to be caught trespassing in a million-dollar villa, so I didn't try and drag him in with me. The first room I searched was the drawing room. It didn't take much intelligence to realise he wasn't there but I checked the huge cupboard there all the same. In my drunken state, I was convinced that Reed, sorry, Mr Reed might try and hide from me, but the cupboard was a particularly unlikely spot – it was just about large enough to hide his drink supply for that week but hardly to conceal a sixteen-stone man.

What, you might wonder, was driving me on to do this daft deed? Drink, as you know, and excitement . . . But also P.J. Wilson, my beloved News Editor back in London. I was convinced I'd never get another foreign assignment if I failed on this one, and I kept remembering his last words to me before I took off from Heathrow: 'Don't bother coming back if you fail!'

Now I was sweeping through all the rooms at a pace that would have impressed the Flying Squad. But still there was no sign of this lumbering giant of the big screen. Then I came to a locked room. It really annoyed me that it was locked and I started pulling the handle up and down in fury. What right I had to be angry I really don't know. After all, here I was virtually breaking and entering someone else's home. All I lacked was a pair of leather gloves and a jemmy.

Something bothered me about this locked room so I bent down and looked through the keyhole. My instincts, as usual, hadn't failed me. There, lying flat on his back on a single bed, was our Mr Reed.

I cannot believe this, I thought to myself. Then the words came out of me defiantly. I must have been completely mad. 'What the fuck are you playing at, Mr Reed? I haven't flown six thousand miles for you to refuse to talk to me.'

He still hadn't moved so much as an inch, so I displayed even more Netherlands-style bravery.

'Everyone wants to know why you've run off with this girl,' I yelled. 'Don't you think it's a bit irresponsible?'

Just as I was thinking what a hypocrite I was, the door burst open. Surprise, surprise. It was Mr Reed, and he was puce with rage. I did the only thing any self-respecting survivor could do – I ran like fucking lightning through the house, with Mr Reed in hot pursuit. He was shouting stuff at me along the lines of 'Her family know all about it,' and 'We are just having a lovely time. It's no business of your's or anyone's,' and 'I don't give a damn what people think,' and 'The lady hasn't been kidnapped.' It was all marvellous stuff, even if it was somewhat unusual for an interview to be conducted as the subject chased the journalist through his own house!

As I emerged on to the porch, clever old Charles had already started up the trusted Mini. In fact I have a sneaking suspicion he was about to piss off and leave me high and dry, but we never bothered broaching the subject as it didn't actually happen. Mr Reed was about five yards behind me, shouting and yelling at the top of his voice as I slammed the Mini door shut and screamed at Charles. 'Let's get the fuck out of here.'

My unhappy snapper was looking frankly horrified, so, as the car screeched out of the driveway, I said to him: 'Welcome to Fleet Street. I suppose we behave a bit differently from the way you do over here.' Charles laughed nervously and sped back (at only twenty-five mph of course) in the direction of the Coconut Grove and my two other punters.

At least thirty minutes had elapsed since I'd left Minder and Josephine to got out for some chicken, but when I walked back into the bar there wasn't a flicker of suspicion in their faces. Minder just seemed relieved to see us because he had bought the last round and didn't like seeing drinks wasted.

Not surprisingly, the evening's fun atmosphere had evaporated somewhat following my absence, and with my two new friends now much sobered up I decided it was nightcap time.

Within half an hour they had wandered off into the night, blissfully unaware of the havoc I had caused back at the villa. I went to my room and fell into a deep sleep within minutes, happy in the knowledge that I'd already got enough in the bag to write a cracking good yarn, as PJ would hopefully call it.

Next morning I was awoken by a call to my room. It was about six and I felt dreadful. The combination of rum punches and jet-lag had certainly taken its toll. 'Hello,' I moaned, wearily convinced it was PJ harassing me for my story.

But no it was Minder. As I heard his voice I felt a definite tingle of fear sliding down my spine.

'Some bastard broke into the villa last night and tried to get an interview with Ollie. He's furious.'

My God, I don't believe my ears, I thought, *he hasn't realised it was me!*

'Do you know if there are any other journalists on the island?' asked Minder.

Despite my throbbing head, it wasn't hard to come up with the right answer.

'Yes, I think there's someone from the *Sunday People* sniffing around,' I answered, lying through my teeth.

'Well, if you see him, tell him he'll get a fucking thrashing if he comes near the villa again.'

It's funny how both drunkenness *and* hangovers make you brave. You'd think one would learn from the other, but it never quite happens that way which is why I asked more than a little naively: 'What about Mr Reed giving me an interview? Then that would kill the story for the others and we could get it all done and out of the way.'

'He wouldn't even give you the fucking time of day, mate,' answered Minder. End of phone conversation.

My next caller was, in fact, PJ. Typically, he wanted me to try for much more from Reed. He was oblivious to the goings-on in Barbados. He just kept saying, 'You haven't got enough yet, matey. We want the works.'

Unbeknown to me, the Fleet Street gossip machine had already got wind of my trip to Barbados. It was probably a combination of pub chat and the fact that we shared a travel agency with our stablemate and deadly rival the *Sunday People*.

I spent the morning pottering around by the pool, wondering if it was madness to try for another chat with Mr Reed and Co. Meanwhile my rival – a freelance reporter based in the States – was experiencing exactly what I was relieved to have avoided on the previous night – in other words, a right old bollocking. I later discovered that the reporter in question innocently arrived at the Reed villa and strolled through the gates just as I had hoped to do sixteen hours earlier. On seeing Mr Reed in the grounds he told him who he was . . . Needless to say, before he could start probing the salient points, Reed and Minder set upon him and chased him down the driveway. One of them was rumoured to be in possession of a meat cleaver at the time, but you know how these stories get exaggerated.

What amused me most was that apparently Reed thought the

man was me – because we had similar features – while Minder thought it must be the 'mystery' intruder from the previous night. All in all I felt pretty pleased with myself. More fool me . . .

By late afternoon I had come to the sober conclusion that there was absolutely no point in pushing my luck and I'd better tell PJ I was still trying to get more from Reed while in fact avoiding him at all costs. As far as I was concerned it was only a matter of time before they put two and two together and worked out it was me who'd raided the villa the night before – remember I knew nothing of the *Sunday People* reporter at this stage. I had even had the good fortune to trace a photograph of Ollie, Josephine and Minder taken by a local restaurant photographer, so I didn't have to worry about making sure Charles got a photo. I told him to wander up and down the beach near the villa and see if he could snatch a shot of the two together, but I wasn't too bothered because I knew I had the whole thing in the bag.

I had just ordered my first rum punch of the day as I sat at the poolside bar when the waiter said there was a call for me. PJ again, no doubt, I thought. Probably going to pile on the pressure just once more. He just couldn't stand the thought of me relaxing and enjoying myself – as if I'd ever do that, I smirked to myself, taking a long sip through a straw.

Fully prepared to tell PJ whatever he wanted to hear, I strolled over to the phone, picked up the receiver and said 'Hello.'

'You little cunt,' came a voice from the other end of the line. It certainly wasn't PJ. 'I'm going to get you unless you get off the island *now*.'

This certainly didn't sound like a Fleet Street executive speaking to one of his reporters. In any case the line was far too clear to be from London. Fucking hell, it was Mr Reed himself. I'd come all this way to talk to him and here he was ringing me at my hotel. I should have been pleased. Instead I was fucking terrified. I needed this call like a hole in the head and I knew it.

'How dare you fucking well break into my home. I'll fucking have you if you come anywhere near me and my friends.'

To say I was petrified would have been the understatement of the century. Then it was Minder's turn.

'Ollie's furious. He knows it was you who came round last night and then this morning he attacked another reporter he thought was you and nearly killed him. You'd better get out quick or else he'll come looking for you.'

Now I was not only shit scared of Reed, I was nervous for my story too. Having a rival on the island was almost as serious as the prospect of being murdered by a raging bull of a film star.

'All he said was that he was from the *People*. If he's one of yours I suggest you advise him to fuck off as well, otherwise this will all turn very nasty,' added Minder.

Bloody hell, he's from the *People*, I thought, that's the worst possible news of all. At least he doesn't seem to have got anything – yet. The phone went dead and, to be frank, I knew how it felt. I feared for my health and I was terrified that the story I'd risked life and limb to get would end up on the front page of every Sunday in Britain. Still, first things first. I had to move fast. Reed and Co knew where I was staying so I had to check out as from now. The hotel manageress thought I was crazy. She was used to tourists booking in for two peaceful weeks of paradise and here I was charging out of the premises after just twenty-four hours, even though on arrival I had assured her I would be staying for at least five days.

Paranoia was now setting in with a vengeance. Before all this frenzy had blown up I had arranged to meet Charles the snapper in an hour's time. I immediately telephoned him and cancelled the meeting, saying there was no need for him to carry on working for me. I had decided I didn't trust him and he might tell Reed where I was going. It was a ludicrous thing to imagine, but when you're feeling paranoid on a strange island you do some silly things.

My next move was to look for a really secluded hotel, somewhere Reed and Co would never dream of looking for me. You may wonder why I didn't just ring PJ and tell him what was going on and get him to pull me back to London. Unfortunately life in Fleet Street just isn't that simple. There was no way I could ring him and admit what was happening. It would be an admission of fear, and in the macho world of tabloid newspapers nobody but nobody gets frightened off.

No, I had to stick it out all on my own. I knew the way to survive the onslaught of Reed and Minder was to keep on the move. I certainly managed that over the following twenty-four hours. I booked into no less than six different hotels – only to check out within hours because people were looking at me strangely in the dining room or the bellboy was acting suspiciously. By the time I had moved into my seventh hotel it began to dawn on me that perhaps I was being a shade paranoid, which is not something that usually dawns on you when you're feeling monumentally paranoid.

I was just walking up the marble steps to the lobby, feeling drained of energy but relieved that I had at last come to terms with my own ridiculous fears, when I heard a bellowing voice:

'He's tall, heavily built and has a moustache . . .'

I stopped in my tracks and saw the unmistakable back of Oliver Reed's head. He was dressed in one of those tropical off-white suits and I could see the beads of sweat running down his neck. *Shit*, I thought, and turned around and ran like greased lightning back down those steps and into my tatty rented Mini-moke jeep. All that paranoia *had* been well founded. Reed himself was doing a hotel-to-hotel check in a furious effort to find me. Jesus, he must be *steaming* . . .

Eventually, after hours of agonised searching, I found a most unlikely spot to lay my weary head. It was a package tour hotel filled to the brim with fat American tourists eating equally fat US-imported barbecue steaks for dinner. I felt secure amongst the hordes of squealing yanks. There was no way Reed would find me here.

All the same, I had a sleepless night. I was worried about Reed; and I had to spin my story together on paper so that I could file it to London first thing the following morning.

I got up at five to phone the article through. With a four-hour time difference I knew I had to get it to London early if I was going to ensure it got in the paper that Sunday.

'Hell-raising actor Oliver Reed has spoken for the first time about his latest leading lady.

'Ollie is holidaying on a sunshine isle with sixteen-year-old schoolgirl Josephine Burge . . .' I filed every comma, dot and spit from my 'on the run' interview with Reed and my drinking session with Josephine and Minder. PJ was deliriously happy, and I managed to get the sort of front-page treatment in the *Sunday Mirror* that every reporter is competing for. It might have been bylined 'From our sweating, terrified, hungover and exhausted man in Barbados', but mercifully it wasn't.

The rest of that Saturday was spent checking in with PJ in London in a token effort to make it look as if I was still working on the story. Let me explain. Every two hours I ring London and say the immortal lines, 'Just checking in, PJ. Any problems?' To which he would always reply, 'Gissa call in a while, mate.' It was his own inimitable way of making sure I was kept on my toes, even though I had filed the story and had little left to do.

At around six that evening I performed what I hoped would be my last check-in call of the week. The only words I wanted to hear now were PJ saying, 'Get the next plane home mate.' Barbados may sound idyllic, but when a film star hunk and his beefy minder are trying to seek and destroy you, it really does make you rather anxious to leave.

'You've done a brilliant job, Wense. The Editor's told me to pass on his congratulations. Well done, mate,' said PJ.

I was delighted. You know what I wanted to hear to round off a momentous chapter . . .

But instead PJ asked me, 'How far are you from Antigua?'

What sort of question was this, I hear you ask. My answer was perplexed to say the least.

'Oh it's at least three islands away, PJ,' I said, without actually having a clue where Antigua was.

'Well, as a reward for doing so well on the Reed story, we'd like you to go and dig up something on the English cricketers who've just arrived in Antigua for the start of their tour of the West Indies.'

My heart sank. Not another beautiful island paradise. I couldn't take the strain. I'd run out of clean clothes, I'd been run ragged by Reed and his henchman, and now was just desperate to get off this fucking island.

'OK, PJ, what exactly do you want me to do?' I asked weakly. My biggest fault in life is that I can never say no. Rather than admit my newly developed loathing for the West Indies, I swallowed my fears and homesickness and headed for the airport to get the next plane to Antigua. It was quite late on Saturday evening by this stage, and I have to say I was just relieved to be getting off the island, even though I wasn't going home to London. The airport seemed strangely empty, but I thought nothing of it as I hurried to the travel inquiries desk to find out the time of the next flight on the infamous island-hopping service that runs between the main Caribbean centres.

Funny, no queue – apart from two European types looking pissed off. I still hadn't added two and two together, though if I'd bothered to look at the departures screens I'd have noticed the dreaded word 'Cancelled'. There was a strike, and I seemed to be the last person in Barbados to have found out about it.

It was the last straw. In fact I'd put it more strongly than that. It was the final nail in my coffin, or so I thought at the time. After half an hour of brain-aching inquiries, I established there was one flight out at six the next morning. There was no way I was going to try and find another hotel to stay in. I'd have to kip at the airport.

It was just then that I noticed a familiar hulk storming into the airport terminal. It was Reed's minder. Not far behind, I truly feared, would be the man himself. I didn't wait to find out, but fled to the gentlemen's – not a pleasant place to hide in a Caribbean airport, I can assure you. For forty dreadful minutes I huddled in a stinking, shit-filled cubicle not daring to move. God knows what all the other regulars at Barbados airport gents thought. I didn't really care about anything except saving my own skin. I'd never felt more paranoid, and never had better reason for it.

When I emerged from my lavatorial hideout, Minder had gone and so had Reed, if he was ever there in the first place. To be quite honest, I'll never be certain whether or not that whole episode was a figment of my imagination, which at the time was entirely controlled by fear.

The next morning I flew off to Paradise Two. It all came to nothing. Even Ian Botham wouldn't talk to me, and by Wednesday I was happily ensconced at my South London home.

But the Ollie Reed story ran and ran. By the Saturday after my return to England, PJ had me and another reporter from the *Sunday Mirror* camped outside Reed's Surrey home. Inside was another *Sunday Mirror* journalist – a rather sexy brunette who was working for us as a freelance. PJ had the 'brilliant idea' of sending this voluptuous creature into the Reed lair to get the penultimate interview on his Caribbean holiday.

But the plan backfired when said reporter knocked on the door on the Friday evening. Eventually she rang PJ and offered to file the real story about 'how wonderful Oliver Reed really is'. At this point Reed himself came on the line and thanked PJ for sending him such a charming scribe. He even said that he had personally dictated every word she was about to file to the *Sunday Mirror* as a 'world exclusive'. We never really found out if it was all an elaborate wind-up by Reed.

But PJ slammed the phone down on him and told colleagues at the *Sunday Mirror* newsdesk: 'She's flipped. I've gone and hired a mad woman as a freelancer. She's finished.' Not a word appeared in the paper the following day, but myself and fellow *Sunday Mirror* man Nick Ferrari were almost run over by Reed and lady hack when they sped out of the drive to his home in a Panther de Ville sports car.

I'll never know if he pointed the car at me deliberately because of my antics in Barbados, but an interesting thing happened when he finally broke his silence about his love for Josephine during an unofficial press conference in his local pub the following week. For when I shouted a question about the romance at him across a crowded saloon bar, he gave me the biggest wink and a smile I've ever seen. It was saying, 'Well played old man.' It was a nice gesture when you consider that this was the man who, not two weeks earlier, had looked very much like he wanted to kill me.

The story had the best possible ending. Some years later Josephine and Reed were married, and have lived happily ever after.

THREE
The Best Doorstep in Britain

IT'S NOT EVERY DAY THAT THE TORY PARTY CHAIRMAN IS exposed as an adulterer and father of an illegitimate lovechild. Revelations about the private life of people in high places invariably get the tabloids buzzing and bring out the best and worst in all of us downmarket hacks. And I was no exception to that rule. It also resulted in the most intense spell of doorstepping – camping outside a subject's home – in my entire journalistic career. It was a classic doorstep, and hacks still dine out on it to this day.

Rumours had been circulating for months about Cecil Parkinson and his love life. Virtually everyone in Fleet Street knew there was one hell of a big skeleton in his closet just waiting, not very patiently, to jump out. The *Daily Mirror* had been shadowing Parkinson's former secretary, Miss Sara Keays, for months after a disgruntled Tory leaked the news that she was pregnant by her lover Cecil. The rest of the Street of Shame just knew there was a major political scandal about to break. We didn't know the details but we knew it was a whopper and couldn't wait to get our hands on it. But the *Daily Mirror* just couldn't seem to crack the story, no matter how hard they tried. Things were not made any easier by Miss Keays' refusal to co-operate with journalists – even though it was clear she had been dumped by Parkinson in favour of his long-suffering wife Ann.

Perhaps Sara Keays was still cherishing the hope that she might get Parkinson to leave loyal Ann. Throughout the summer of 1983 she was constantly badgered by reporters from the

Daily Mirror, but in a classic example of undying loyalty she refused to crack. In some ways, Miss Keays was acting more like the wife than the mistress. To the journalists involved it no doubt seemed an extraordinary stance to take.

But in September, with the Tory Party Conference fast approaching, the news finally hit the front page of the *Mirror* – and that opened the floodgates for the rest of us. It was a sensational story. But Miss Keays remained determined not to speak publicly about their affair and the impending birth of a child. That was why, even when the story was about to break, no one actually got Miss Keays to talk about it. This was like throwing down the gauntlet to Fleet Street, and it was a challenge that every paper felt obliged to take up. We all wanted to be the first to have an exclusive chat with this rather stern looking woman who'd suddenly been catapulted into the world headlines. Figures ranging between £100,000 and £1 million were being bandied around in a frenzied attempt to persuade Miss Keays to open up her heart. But these astronomical figures were falling on deaf ears.

All contact with her had to go through her solicitor, Mr Geoffrey Wicks. Now lawyers and journalists don't often see eye to eye. Bland statements were issued in the hope that they would put Fleet Street off the scent, but in reality all they did was fuel our interest even more. Miss Keays was herself being photographed everywhere she went. To start with she looked as if she was positively enjoying all the attention, but as time progressed and all her family and friends were beginning to be pestered, she became – understandably – irritable and grumpy with all the hacks who haunted her every move. Public opinion was firmly on her side at this stage – she was the wronged woman, and Cecil the villain of the piece.

Her sister's flat in Battersea and her parent's home in Wiltshire were under constant siege from us all. Yet still Miss Keays resisted all temptation to speak openly. Whenever she did utter anything it was furiously scribbled down by the pursuing pack. Fascinating statements like 'I'm going out to dinner with friends for the evening' were making front-page news. All in all, it was getting more than a mite ridiculous. But none of us were going to give up the hunt. Tearing a politician's reputation to pieces, especially one of Margaret Thatcher's favourites, was just what we liked doing best.

It was no surprise when the lovable P.J. Wilson hailed me over to the newsdesk one dreary Thursday afternoon, just after the Parkinson scandal had exploded. 'Off you go, mate,' he barked. He didn't mention where I was supposed to be going – it was all a PJ test to see if I'd read that day's papers. Sometimes working on the *Sunday Mirror* was a bit like being back at school. 'I want you to go down to the dad's house. She'll turn up there sooner or later. Bound to.'

This was pure guesswork, but PJ's instincts often proved absolutely spot on. With me on this expedition were fellow reporter Greg Miskiw and a young lady freelance. Despite the Oliver Reed disaster, PJ still held the old-fashioned belief that a woman would stand the best chance of getting an interview with another woman.

It was just like old times as I drove down the M4, scene of so many journeys during the Royal Train story. The weather was appalling, it was bucketing down, and the Keays' mansion was not an easy place to find. Situated on the edge of a fairly ordinary village called Marksbury, it was not what I would call the perfect doorstep by any means.

Doorsteps are an essential ingredient of life on the road with a tabloid newspaper. (The name originated because in the old days you would literally stand on the doorstep waiting for an interview. These days it's become slightly more refined as most journalists have cars.) They can vary enormously. You might end up on a doorstep outside a block of council flats and that is, quite frankly, a nightmare. It is impossible to see who's coming or going and that makes it pretty difficult to trap your prey. The problem with the Keays' house as far as doorstepping was concerned was that it was on a main road. That meant if there were too many hacks loitering around we'd end up blocking the traffic and the police would appear on the scene and ask us to move on.

Not surprisingly, every single newspaper from the *Star* to the *Guardian* was represented on this doorstep – and normally in triplicate. That meant that the area immediately at the end of the Keays' driveway was thronged with journalists, at least forty of them. Not a pretty sight by anyone's standards, unless you happen to be Joan Collins about to launch a new brand of perfume. Myself and my two *Sunday Mirror* colleagues sat conspicuously in our staff car on a muddy verge opposite the entrance to the house. Greg Miskiw and I settled down to do what journalists like most of all – have a good gossip. At that stage we were just happy to have got out of the office. We didn't really care that there was little chance of ever interviewing this woman. She was hardly likely to pour out her heart to a crowd of rain-soaked hacks. But we were all there just in case she did. It was daft, really, but fear breeds all sorts of silly decisions in Fleet Street. No News Editor could afford to take the risk that he or she might miss out if Miss Keays suddenly cracked outside her father's house.

Our female companion – who was relatively new to the game – sat quietly in the back of the car as we talked, and talked, and talked – about everything other than the matter at hand. We knew the chances of getting anywhere that night were getting more remote by the minute. And then suddenly a grey-haired, bespectacled man walked down from the house to the gates.

There was pandemonium. Forty bored, hungry hacks surged forward towards him. Greg and I jumped out of the car and rushed for the gates. We didn't want to miss out on the fun.

'Why can't you just leave us alone. Go away. We don't want to talk to you. Please leave us in peace.'

The old man was Sara's father and he had obviously had enough. The amazing thing was that virtually every daily newspaperman present was taking down every word as he spoke. Yet all he was doing – in his own gentlemanly way – was telling us all to bugger off.

Greg and I looked at each other in disbelief – and relief. The last thing we wanted at that stage was the father speaking in any detail to anyone. After all, it was Thursday evening and the dailies still had two more days of publication before our paper came out. As Sunday men we were very much on the defensive.

The old man disappeared within minutes and Greg and I, having exhausted all our mutual gossip, decided it was time to get down to work. The very fact that forty-odd scribes were present was an opportunity in itself, and the first thing a Sunday newspaperman should do when he arrives on the scene of a mass doorstep like this is talk to the daily boys. That's the quickest short-cut to gathering information about a running story like Parkinson. They've got nothing to lose by telling you what they know since they've always got tomorrow's paper to publish in while you've got to wait till Sunday.

It was with this news-gathering method in mind that I toured the Keays encampment. Chatting casually to old friends from the *Mail*, the *Mirror* and *The Sun*, I soon established certain details that would have taken me days to track down on my own. Greg did exactly the same with his mates. By the time we both returned to our car, we had enough background info to call it a day and retire to dine at the most expensive restaurant we could find in nearby Bristol.

Over dinner Greg and I – with our female colleague still taking a quiet back seat – wondered how we were going to get at least one world exclusive on the Sara Keays story the next day. As we settled back in our comfortable seats at Harvey's Restaurant (£50 a head even in those far off days) and drank the finest port, we ran through our best leads. We knew Miss Keays had a brother who lived nearby. We also had a number for a cousin, plus a load of names and addresses for friends who lived near the Wiltshire mansion. All this info had come from our friends on the dailies, but they'd never had the time to develop these leads. One of the great things about working on a Sunday paper is that you have got the time. The downside is that you may have to conjure up a revelation when one doesn't really exist, because you are obliged to provide a good follow-up story on a national scandal.

Eventually Greg and I and our female hand returned to our respective rooms at the Holiday Inn Bristol for a good night's sleep – happy in the knowledge that we had enough to cause some trouble the next day.

We were all up at the crack of dawn and travelled over to the doorstep just to make sure there hadn't been any overnight developments. Nothing had changed, except that those reporters who'd actually been mug enough to sleep the night in their cars parked at the country's biggest doorstep now looked distinctly stiff and bedraggled. At this juncture, Greg and I decided it was time to dump our still taciturn female colleague. We left her shivering outside the gates to *chez* Keays.

'Make sure you keep in touch with the news desk if there are any movements,' I told her. Without a car to sit in, it was going to be a wet and windy day for that particular hackette.

A tour of Wiltshire's lesser known beauty spots followed. First port of call was the home of a farm worker who had known Sara all her life. Driving into the muddy farmyard, I guess I should have known better than to start nosing around in a tightly-knit rural community, but as a city boy through and through I didn't really give it enough thought.

'What do you want?' asked a rough-looking son of the soil as we got out of our car, looking highly conspicuous in Burberry raincoats and ties undone at the top button.

'We were just wondering if we could speak to you privately?' I replied gently but with an air of firmness.

It was a doorstep technique I had used on many previous occasions. I wouldn't go so far as to say I was impersonating an officer of the law . . . It's just that if you are six feet tall, well built and wearing a suit and you turn up at a complete stranger's house uninvited and wanting to have a private word, there's a good chance you'll be mistaken for one of our beloved boys in blue. My partner Greg looked equally convincing, if a little on the short side. This farm worker fell for it, anyway.

Once inside the messy front room of the farmhouse, I started with a few basic police-style questions, waiting for him to ask exactly who we were.

But he never did. Instead he told us some boring stuff about what a nice little girl Sara had always been and how he didn't believe a word he had read in the newspapers because 'they always make everything up, don't they?' At this point I realised that, despite our success in gaining entry to his house, we were getting nowhere fast. So I gave Greg a subtle hint and off we went, having given our bucolic friend a lecture on how untrustworthy the tabloids were. I wanted to ensure that no other clever dick hacks persuaded him to talk and reveal more than he had done to us. That would make us look very bad indeed.

We had managed to get exactly what we did not want – a glowing tribute to Sara Keays from a farmhand who wasn't even sure how to pronounce Parkinson's name and certainly didn't have much idea who he was. It was all most unsatisfactory, so Greg and I headed for the nearest hostelry and decided to do some in-depth research into the Keays' drinking habits.

Supping an essential pint of research, Greg and I got talking to the landlord of the pub and – in common with the rest of the world – he turned out to be an authority on Miss Keays. Once again, we both omitted to mention that we were reporters, and carried on instead with the officers-of-the-law impression that had worked so well with the farm worker earlier. Soon we were in possession of some new leads – names of some of Sara's friends, some gossip about the local grocery shop, and a host of other titbits of the kind that might – or might not – help keep the *Sunday Mirror* on the news-stands.

Satisfied that we had bled our new best friend dry, Greg and I headed off in pursuit of all these incredibly important links in the chain. We were feeling very high from a combination of drink and achievement – the achievement being that we thought we had some very hot Keays contacts in our possession.

It was an almighty disaster. Every single person we went to see either threatened us with a shotgun or tried to call the police. It was extraordinary how loyal the whole community was being towards Miss Keays and her as yet unborn child. But then I should have seen it coming. This neighbourhood had all the tell-tale signs of anti-tabloid territory.

It was a feeling I regularly got as a member of the popular press – unpopular would be more accurate. I remember doorstepping a woman in Hull who had been exposed as a paedophile. During the court case it had emerged that she made ten year old boys perform bizarre sexual acts in front of her and her husband in their neat little bungalow just a stone's throw from the docks. The case made headline news all around the country and caused special outrage as it seemed to break down the most basic boundaries of human decency. Anyway, that's how the editorial in one not entirely virtuous rag put it. You would have thought the couple's neighbours would be just as horrified by their activities – after all, this bizarre couple had been sexually molesting schoolchildren inside their own community. So when I arrived in this windswept seaport, notebook in hand, I was – understandably – expecting an easy ride from the residents who lived nearby. Not a bit of it. Not one of the twenty other red-brick-built one-storey homes in the street was inhabited by someone who would say a bad word about their appalling, depraved neighbours. 'Why don't you go home and leave us all alone?' was the most common reply to a charming doorstep approach from yours truly. One woman even tried to set her Alsatian on me. I decided there and then that she must have taken part in some of these sick orgies. Why else should she defend these people? Maybe the dog joined in as well.

But the response I got had nothing to do with local feeling about the couple. The truth is that snooping hacks are guaranteed to inspire a fit of neighbourly solidarity. When the tabloids swoop on a street or village, the whole community tends to take them on, irrespective of the dirty deeds that might have been committed by their fellow residents. It is us versus them. Whether one of their number is Jack the Ripper or Jack and the Beanstalk doesn't seem to matter.

It is fascinating the way the press spark off such fanatical emotions in people. When the pack turns up on a doorstep, ranks are closed and that's that. I mean, most of the villagers I was interviewing about Miss Keays would have gone potty if their daughter had come home one day and said she was pregnant by her married lover, but when it came to protecting one in their midst, tribal instincts took over.

Back in Marksbury, Wiltshire, journalistic instincts were taking over. It was late afternoon Friday and Greg and I hadn't got a sausage. Not a bean. Not even a morsel to offer PJ so that we could go off duty and enjoy another gourmet meal. What made it worse was that I had earmarked somewhere in Bath that was starred in the Michelin guide. We could think of nothing better to do than return to the Keays mansion and join the rest of the hounds, who looked just as pissed off as we felt. A few new faces had joined the pack, so we decided to pump them for a new lead. I spotted a young bloke from a local news agency whom I'd spoken to a few times in the past. The great thing about local agencies is that they are normally manned by keen young hacks anxious to impress the big boys from London. In my language, that meant I might squeeze a new line out of this guy without him realising. The whole of Britain is scattered with news agencies. They are often managed by former Fleet Street operators and they work for whoever pays them – a bit like bounty hunters in the old wild west. They cover most of the courts and local council meetings and always, without fail, turn up at doorsteps like this one.

I began my approach to this particular young agency hound in the traditionally casual manner.

'How's things, mate?'

'Oh, fine. This is a right fucking bore, isn't it?'

Five minutes of similarly uninteresting conversation followed before we got onto the subject at hand. I soon realised that this pup was delighted even to be seen talking to one of the Fleet Street boys. All his mates from other agencies were looking at us and wondering what we were talking about. 'Maybe they're in league with the *Sunday Mirror*? Do you think they've bought someone up?' These are the sort of questions that would have been going through their minds as I stood chatting with my new friend about nothing more important than the weather.

However, slowly but surely I was edging towards some useful info. I was well aware he had the address of Sara Keays' brother, and I wanted to find out if he'd got anything worth- while out of him. But I had to go carefully so that he wouldn't realise what I was after.

'Seen the brother yet?' I asked with a yawn.

'Yeah. He's a waste of time. Everyone's had a go at him but he won't say a word.'

'Did you all doorstep him then?'

'Yeah, on Wednesday night. He got right pissed off.'

'What did he do? Threaten you with the cops?'

'No. He was quite civilised towards us, but didn't want to give an interview. After about five minutes of pleading with him we all went on our way.'

As far as I was concerned, this was getting interesting. I now knew that the brother had spent a few minutes actually talking to the pack – something the daily boys had kept from me on my first circuit of the encampment. But nothing had appeared in the papers so obviously they'd all thought it wasn't worth quoting in a story. Now, even though it was forty-eight hours since that doorstep had taken place, I was trying to extract from this young rookie the precise quotes. The reason was that daily paper journalists think in a different way from Sunday hacks. As far as they are concerned, if the quotes they get are not relevant to that particular day's events, then they don't bother saving them for use later on during a running story like the Parkinson affair. But I knew the value of any quotes, especially if they hadn't been used and might turn into good leads.

'What sort of stuff did the brother have to say?' I went on.

'Not much. Just why don't you go away. All the normal stuff.'

'But he must have said something?'

'Oh, he just muttered something about how she was still in love with Parkinson. But we knew that anyway, didn't we?'

(Breakthrough!) 'Oh. Were you all there, then?' I asked, trying to sound bored.

'I am not sure. Actually, I think it was just me and a bloke from the local rag who'd hung on just in case.'

This was just what I'd been waiting for. I pumped the pup further, got all the quotes he had, thanked him (not too profusely in case he smelt a rat) and wandered back to Greg in the car. It looked like the main pack had left the brother's doorstep just a few minutes too early – even better, the agency hacks seemed not to understand the value of what they'd got hold of by hanging on for those vital extra minutes. I was a happy and relieved man. Now we could get to that restaurant in time for last orders.

Contrary to popular belief, most newspaper stories are gathered in precisely the way I have just described: journalists talking to other journalists. My main task on the Saturday morning was to try and confirm what I had with the brother but I never did get through to him, so I wrote the story based on second-hand quotes. That Sunday I scooped the rest of the Sunday tabloids with a front-page story headlined: SARA STILL LOVES HIM – SAYS BROTHER. I wonder what the pup thought when he read it . . .

But my involvement with Parkinson doorsteps didn't end there. The story ran and ran for months. It was the biggest political scandal of the decade – even though Parkinson has now been forgiven and is back in the corridors of power. Anyway, the week following my adventures in Wiltshire at the Keays' house were spent at the Hertfordshire mansion of the man himself. This time there were about sixty of us camped outside the Parkinson home near the fascinating town of Potters Bar.

It was intriguing to compare the two women in the life of Romeo Parkinson. Having spent the previous week witnessing the comings and goings of Sara and her family, here I was watching Cecil and his wife. They often say that men pick mistresses who remind them of their wives and this was definitely the case as far as the Tory Party Chairman was concerned. Both women were dark haired, attractive if not beautiful, and from good family backgrounds. Even the way they dressed (though there was a considerable age gap) was similar. And they both treated the press with utter contempt whenever we went anywhere near them. Here I was in damp Hertfordshire being given the same sort of icy stare of hatred that I'd got less than a week earlier – but this time it was from Ann not Sara.

What made this doorstep considerably worse than the Wiltshire version was the fact that everyone was convinced Cecil would have to make a statement about his future in the Cabinet that week. That meant we all had to sleep in our cars overnight outside the house because we were fearful that Cecil might pop out to walk the dog at the crack of dawn and reveal all in passing.

The first day I was there passed off without incident. I couldn't even skim a good line from any of the assembled hacks because we were so near to London that all the big boys were present and there were no friendly local agency guys around to help me in my usual plight. In fact, so little was happening that the massive press presence was making more TV news than Parkinson's predicament. With the man himself in hiding, the cameras had to make do with shots of us lot camped outside his home. Some of my friends in London even rang my home to say they'd seen me on the telly. Sadly, I wasn't there to take their calls as I was still glued to Mr Parkinson's front door. Things were gradually becoming very icy between Mrs P and her two daughters and the assembled pack. One of the daughters told us all to go away before her mother opened the front door and pulled her inside. Tempers were fraying. It was hardly the sort of display of emotion that Mr Cool Cecil would approve of. He was, and still is, the epitome of good manners and charm. Dare I say it, there are times when he really is too good to be true. I suppose that's why, in our naivety, we all thought he might crack and give us some sort of interview. But he obviously hadn't sent his family to the same charm school he had attended and, not surprisingly, they were getting fed up with having sixty people in their front garden.

The weather is a crucial factor during lengthy doorsteps and for the first forty-eight hours of my stay outside the Parkinson home it was sunny and reasonably mild. That was bad news for the long-suffering Mrs P, because the better the weather the longer the hounds will hang around. Still, we were all getting extremely bored. As usual, we were the victims of anxious News Editors terrified of pulling us off in case Cecil decided to open up his heart – a highly unlikely occurrence, but most News Editors are, as I've said before, eternal optimists, other- wise they wouldn't be any good at their jobs. No one was going to leave this doorstep until a newspaper executive back in London had the courage to realise it was a complete waste of time and send his man home. Then all the others would follow suit.

By Friday evening I would have killed for a hot meal, a steaming bath and a feather bed – or any bed for that matter. It was pitch dark outside the house and the lone policeman on duty had long since stopped talking to any of us for fear he'd end up being quoted on the next day's front page – there was that little fresh news about the Parkinson affair around.

Out of the murk, a Mini Metro screeched past the front of the house and came to a halt about thirty yards up the road. I noticed a couple of hacks running towards it. What on earth was going on? None of the Parkinsons drove a Metro, and Mrs T would hardly turn up in one, would she? I got out of my car to investigate. The ITN man had turned on his spotlight and there, eerily lit up against a black background, were the haggard features of Mr Norman Tebbit. It was a bizarre scene to say the least. Our Norman looked furious as we all rapidly cottoned on to what was happening and rushed – all sixty of us – towards him. The first thing he did was carefully lock his car. It was a strange response to a mob of news-hungry hacks – as if he thought we might nick it. And the way we felt by then I guess we might have done, just to relieve the tedium. Lit up by this incredibly strong TV beam, he didn't look a happy man. He was fuming, steaming with rage. It was not a pretty sight, I can assure you.

During this period, Norman was very much the Tory hard

man. No one dared upset him and he had a reputation for giving a hard time to anyone who got in his way. He was seen as one of Maggie's top lieutenants – a ruthless troubleshooter, tirelessly aggressive in the Party cause. He was also said to be an old chum of Cecil's. But on this occasion he was, for a few moments at least, speechless. He seemed shocked and horrified that we were all camped outside the Parkinson abode. There was a look of disgust and contempt on his face when one keen young hack asked him: 'Do you think Mr Parkinson should resign as Chairman?' His anger was there for all to see.

As he walked towards the front door, we followed his every movement. It must have been a strange sight, like something out of Monty Python – sixty grown men and women stalking this lone figure as if engaged in a game of Grandmother's footsteps. Each time he stopped we stopped with him. If only he'd say something . . . But though his lips were pursed and quivering with anger, not a word was forthcoming.

He was now just ten yards from the Parkinson house, lit up like Dracula in a 1930s film – very much a silent movie, but without the benefit of a musical accompaniment.

Then another poor innocent hack cast forth: 'Do you think an adulterer should remain in the Cabinet?'

It was all too much for our Norman. He lost those ice-cool airline-pilot nerves of his and exploded: 'I don't talk to jumped up pygmies. Go away.' It was a remarkable outburst from a senior member of Mrs T's team. And as he turned and walked to the front door, which conveniently opened for him at that very moment, one witty scribe started imitating an ape – and then the whole load of us joined in. Hardly the way to treat a senior politician, you might say. But the joke was on us because half the hacks obviously thought a pygmy was an animal!

Norman emerged from the Parkinson home in the early hours. He was saying nothing, and since most of us were dozing in our vehicles we didn't take much notice of him. His performance earlier that evening had proved he wasn't worth pursuing.

The next morning started badly because it was pissing down

with rain. I had spent another incredibly uncomfortable night in the front seat of my Mirror Group Triumph Acclaim. The Parkinsons must have been delighted with the downpour – perhaps it meant we would all go away and leave them in peace. Maybe the church-going Mrs P saw it as a gift from the Heavens. All sixty of us miserable hacks certainly didn't. By eleven we were all drenched to the skin. Absurdly, the only reason we were all so wet was that we had to keep in constant touch with our offices, and that meant a hundred-yard walk down the road to the only telephone box in the area. In the early eighties carphones were a rarity, and if one of our number had had one, we'd have mobbed him.

By this stage it wasn't just pouring, it was coming down in torrents – you know the sort of thing, open the window a crack to let some air in and you get the Niagara Falls instead. Then, just when it seemed we'd all be swept away by the world's first tidal wave, the front door of the Parkinson home opened and out stepped the man himself. He was carrying a tray with two bottles of finest malt whisky. He looked like an off-duty maitre d' from the Savoy. All the mannerisms were there: charm, poise, perfectly groomed hair and clothes – except he had on his Saturday-at-home-with-the-family sweater and cords.

What on earth is happening, I thought as Cecil walked towards our muddy camp. Is he going to chuck the lot at us in a final gesture of defiance for the way we had harassed him and his family? Or maybe he was taking the scotch down the road to a local fête to give away as a prize in a raffle? Cecil was staying tight-lipped. Now he was walking towards his lock-up garage with these most unlikely props. He put the tray down, and calmly opened the huge swing doors to expose a completely empty garage.

'I thought you might like some refreshment and shelter from this terrible weather,' said Cec in a calm, strong voice.

We rushed in to the garage anxious for two things – a swig of whisky and the chance of a chat with Parkinson, in that order.

Sixty people crammed into a garage near twee Potters Bar, trying desperately to get their hands on a paper cup (he'd even remembered to bring them out) full of finest malt. But there the interview of the year ended, for Cec didn't utter another word. He just disappeared through the back of the garage into his rear garden.

We were all flabbergasted. Here was the Tory Chairman, about to be the father of a lovechild by his former secretary, entertaining hordes of Fleet Street hacks in his garage. It was an extraordinary move on Parkinson's part. As far as us cynical scribes were concerned, it was just him trying to win us over. Tabloid reporters believe in the old adage 'You don't get owt for nowt.' What was he after? Did he really think we'd let him off lightly because he'd given us a free drink and his garage to shelter in? What member of staff at Tory HQ had dreamed up this one, we asked ourselves.

The truth was probably that he just felt a bit sorry for us, knowing we were only doing our jobs and acting on orders from above. But I must admit, I did think it was a typically well calculated gesture from a man who had – until recently – cornered the market in political self-promotion. And sure enough, as soon as most of us had filed the non-story about how nice Mr P had been to us all, our News Editors pulled us off the doorstep and we all went home empty handed. I thought at the time – and still do – that Parkinson's ploy worked a treat from his point of view.

Shortly after the Parkinson fiasco, I found myself involved in a story that illustrates a totally different sort of doorstepping assignment.

Certain personalities become famous by dint of hard work and achievement, some by doing outrageous things, and some just by becoming the object of a tabloid obsession. One such character is George Best. There can be no doubt he was a fine soccer player in his day, but that was fifteen years ago. And though he's achieved plenty on the football pitch, that can't explain why even now – in his mid to late forties – he still gets enormous amounts of coverage for the most banal things. His personal life has always been turned over and over by the tabloids, and really, because he was once an anti-establishment tearaway, it is Fleet Street that has made him a character worthy of Fleet Street's attention. Whatever George did, the newspapers were there to report. No one ever bothered to ask poor old George whether he minded, and in fact he sometimes gave the impression of needing all the coverage he could get.

So, when he was imprisoned for drunken driving and assaulting a police officer, it was hardly surprising that every tabloid in town was after a good story about George Best's life inside jail. I and what seemed like hundreds of other Fleet Street hacks were dispatched to a sleepy area of East Sussex, where playboy George was doing porridge in Ford Open Prison. At first glance it didn't seem like a very hospitable location for a doorstep. The land surrounding the prison was flat and bleak. It was January and there wasn't even a bus shelter to gather under. When I arrived, many of the hacks had already been hanging around for days and looked thoroughly pissed off. They had spent all their time trying to grab a few words with totally uncooperative prison guards and inmates who had just been released.

I knew the *Sunday Mirror* would keep me down there for at least three days, so I decided to make sure it was as comfy as possible. My News Editor had very considerately let me have two assistants and I immediately left them both at the jail while I went off on more important business.

Just before leaving the office a few hours earlier, I had asked around in case anyone knew a good hotel in the vicinity of Ford. One bright spark said he'd taken his girlfriend to a really olde worlde place just a few miles from the prison. The fact that he had been there for pleasure rather than business made me sceptical, but I decided to make that particular hotel my first port of call. You may wonder why I wasn't doing my bit and talking to inmates and officers at Ford. Simple. I knew there was no point until I had found us a good hostelry. How could I – or my troops – operate at full effectiveness if we didn't know where we were going to end up that night? I had long since passed the stage where I was prepared to risk it and just fall into the first hotel I could find after a hard day on a doorstep. The hotel came first, the story second. I could think of nothing worse than ending up in some rotting dive that didn't even have a phone. After all the *Mirror* was paying so why not get the best? The way I saw it I was protecting the paper's interests by making sure the team's morale was high and they were fit and ready for action at all times.

Anyway, the hotel recommended by my colleague turned out to be perfect. It had rooms with baths, telephones and even cable TV. But most important of all, it had a great little bar. With the first stage of my mission accomplished, I checked us all in and headed back to dreary Ford and the dozens of hacks waiting for any scrap of information about our Georgie.

With fifty mph winds howling round our ankles and a definite lack of punters to harass, we soon came to the conclusion that it was time to retire to the warm comforts of our hotel. Unlike our hapless daily paper colleagues, we could afford to eat, drink and be merry and still file our story by Saturday morning. And that was precisely what myself and one of my two assistants were doing. The other one – whom I wasn't so friendly with – was left to guard the prison just in case George tried to escape or some other such unlikely drama.

That evening was spent in the company of a hilarious barmaid called Ethel – who was in her sixties and, following a hefty five-course dinner, introduced the assembled press corps to a vast array of lethal cocktails. The pick of them was an extraordinary mixture that went by the highly suggestive name of a 'Purple Fucker'. I don't actually know what was in it, but it certainly seemed to do the trick. By four in the morning there were only three of us left and we all drank a toast to 'poor old Georgie'. After all, not only was he in jail just up the road but he was a self-confessed alcoholic as well.

The next day was spent in a hungover haze made all the more difficult to handle by a suggestion from one of my two assistants. He was insisting (perhaps naively or perhaps bravely) that one of us should try and break *into* the prison and get a chat with Georgie.

Now that might sound about as idiotic a scheme as any you have ever heard of. But it didn't seem that way to me when I sat and considered it on that cold, drizzly, January day. Ford was, after all, an open prison, and inmates were able to walk freely around the grounds. In addition, the prison was split into two sections by a main road which, believe it or not, the prisoners had to cross every time they went from their dormitories to the recreation areas. It was a strange sight, watching inmates walking casually across a busy road as if they were just ordinary people out for a stroll. Anyway, our master plan was that one of us should hang around when a crowd of prisoners crossed the road, try and mingle in with them, and then slip past the guards at a particularly busy moment.

At first I pointed out that this could cause a major problem with the prison authorities. Then my trusted assistant pointed out that we were breaking *into* jail, not out, so what offence could we be committing? It was a daft argument, but my ever-increasing hangover couldn't handle the idea of a long discussion about it, so I gave one of my assistants the nod to go ahead and try. I should have known better.

It was getting close to lunchtime and we knew a load of inmates would come out any minute to walk across the road from their dormitories to the refectory. As we stood huddled near the prison entrance, a group of prisoners came bounding across the road. I pushed my assistant towards them and whispered: 'You're on your own, mate.'

He walked into the crowd blissfully unaware that what I meant was that I would deny ever sending him inside if the shit hit the fan. I think he thought I was just using a bit of dramatic terminology. I watched discreetly as the foolhardy newshound shuffled in amongst the evil-looking selection of cons. As they crossed the road he seemed to have cracked it. He looked like one of them – luckily they were allowed to wear their own clothes at Ford.

I turned to my other assistant and said: 'Jammy fucker. He seems to be on his way in.'

The other hacks looked on in amazement at the sheer gall of

my colleague. However, the *Sunday Mirror* plant seemed to have hit on a problem. As the crowd of prisoners swept into the entrance, I noticed my man fall to the ground. Within seconds the group had disappeared into the prison grounds.

Our man nearly inside Ford Prison was left in a heap on the ground and he didn't look too well at all. I rushed over to him and helped him to his feet. He was ruffled to say the least.

'Bastards tripped me up and then started muttering "Press scum. Leave our George alone."'

It was crystal clear that our George had some meaty friends on the inside. But it was a crazy scheme in the first place and deserved to fail. Ironically, another more artful hack managed to get round the back of the prison grounds some days later and snapped some great photos of George which ended up being splashed across a rival Sunday paper.

But that's the way it goes, I guess.

FOUR
Not Bloody Likely

IN JANUARY 1982, AN INCIDENT OCCURRED THAT PROBABLY had a more profound effect on Prime Minister Margaret Thatcher than any war, economic crisis or domestic disaster.

She and her Tory stalwarts were riding high in the political charts at the time. Branded the 'Iron Lady' by the Russians, she was building up a reputation as an unrivalled world leader, while on the home front the Labour Party was in disarray, with Michael Foot struggling to preserve any semblance of unity. Yuppies were coming out of the woodwork – Golf GTis and BMW 3 series were flooding the roads. It was a time of great prosperity all round and most newspapers were telling us it was all thanks to our Maggie (isn't it interesting the way she is no longer referred to by her Christian name?). But then Mark Thatcher got involved in an escapade that nearly flushed all his mother's effort and success down the pan.

Very little was known about Mark up until Mrs T's election in 1979. His twin sister Carol had enjoyed more coverage, thanks to a career in radio journalism (despite having a lisp), and later newspapers. She also got involved in a number of relationships, which tended to be splashed all over the papers she didn't write for. Carol was liked by many in Fleet Street. She had made brave efforts to break into journalism and got a number of freelance travel assignments in a variety of publications. I don't ever recall her visiting the Sahara Desert, though. If she had then perhaps she would have advised Mark against his disastrous trip there and saved us all a lot of trouble.

In the two years leading up to January 1982, Mark had had a variety of jobs but seemed intent on entering the car sales field. Perhaps it was not the ideal job for a Prime Minister's child, but he was mad keen on motor racing so it seemed to make sense. And, so the rumours went, it was the perfect way of keeping him out of harm's way. The Thatcher entourage was eager to keep her image as clean as possible.

We'd all been treated to a delightful set of photos showing the Thatchers relaxing (royal style, of course) at Chequers at Christmas. They looked the perfect family unit, but boy Mark was hiding a secret from the world as he sat in that delightful Yuletide scene. He had defied family advice and entered the notoriously dangerous Paris to Dakar motor rally. This time the boy racer inside him had got the better of him. Mummy and Daddy must have been appalled. Their son was about to risk life and limb in the desert amongst all those foreigners. It was too horrible a thought to contemplate.

But up to that point we journalists had not really taken poor old Mark seriously and that, I suspect, is precisely why he took up the gauntlet. Within days of the announcement, we were being fed a constant diet of Hero Mark type stories. Maybe the trip wasn't such a bad idea after all? Mark was beginning to look like a creditable chip off the old Iron Lady block during the build-up to the rally. Dressed in an immaculate white all-in-one racing boiler suit, photographs of Mark preparing for the 'biggest race of my life' were appearing in every paper. He looked every inch the macho hero. It was all good old-fashioned stuff and Mark, not surprisingly, seemed to be revelling in all the attention. His warm-up races were getting as much attention as most Grands Prix and, as we were soon to find out, he had another surprise up his perfect white cotton sleeve. For the papers discovered that he was actually co-driving with a beautiful Frenchwoman throughout the rally. Soon there were rumours of a romance that would probably boost Anglo-French relationships no end.

It now had all the perfect ingredients: glamour, fast cars, Prime Minister's son – what more could a good publicity man want? If only he had sought advice from a fortune-teller . . .

The start of the rally in Paris got mass coverage. Mark and his gorgeous companion looked made for each other as they spoke in deadly serious terms about winning the race. The only slight problem was Mark's inability to smile. It was definitely something he found difficult to do in front of journalists. But his attractive companion successfully deflected the cameras. Dressed in sexy, tight-fitting outfits and clearly not short of Gallic arrogance, she certainly looked the part. It was fairly clear to all who was going to be in charge of this particular jaunt.

While all this was going on, I was just a humble observer back in London, with nothing but a passing interest in seeing the outcome of this adventure. In common with many in Britain at the time, I was irritated that this guy was getting so much publicity because of who his mother was. It seemed all wrong to me. But I wasn't going to lose any sleep over it. There were many much more important things in life to worry about.

By the middle of that week, I think the whole nation was already beginning to feel the same way. After all, Mark was only driving through Europe on roads that you or I might use every year. At each check-in point, TV and press cameras were there to capture his every emotion. It was all grossly over-the-top – much like the Richard Branson stunts that became so famous long after the dust had settled on Mark's adventures.

MARK GETS ON FERRY! MARK AND HIS GIRL SWITCH ON ENGINE. MARK DRIVES DOWN ROAD. Those weren't the actual headlines, but they might as well have been.

Soon reports were reaching the papers and TV of Mark's amazing bravery in North Africa, where it was claimed he was in a very strong position (with the car, that is). The nation was fed pictures of him speeding through the desert sand with blonde beauty at his side. Mark the wonder boy in action. Looking as debonair as ever, he seemed to be trying to cast himself as the lead in the next remake of *Lawrence of Arabia*.

Meanwhile, I was just starting the week at the *Sunday Mirror* with, as was often the case, very little in the way of good stories on the horizon. I had begun work on the Wednesday because we were only working a four-day week at the time. Four-day weeks were a wonderful relic of the closed-shop era in Fleet

Street, when the unions dominated. I guess that it was no surprise when Messrs Maxwell and Murdoch abolished all those cosy working practices. The only thing I had managed to do by the end of the day was to work out my expenses for the previous three weeks – no mean achievement, I can assure you. It seemed a dead week from a domestic news point of view, with Mark hogging all the limelight in the most sickening fashion.

That night, ITN featured yet more shots of macho Mark on the early evening bulletin. But by the time News at Ten came on, the story had changed dramatically. 'Mark Thatcher feared lost in desert.' (*Bong*) 'Mrs Thatcher breaks down in tears.' (*Bong*) 'She may fly to Algeria to help search for her son.' (*Bong*) This was the gist of it, even if those weren't exact words. Then Mrs T was pictured close to grief by the ITN cameras. It was a human side to our tough-talking leader that few realised existed. Meanwhile, boy Mark was somewhere in the Sahara looking for an oasis . . .

Next morning I drove across South London listening to LBC Radio's update on the crisis. Rumours were still abounding that our PM might fly out to the desert to supervise this media event in person. When I walked into the newsroom, P.J. Wilson was looking decidedly edgy, and I could guess what assignment was on his mind. I was the first one in apart from him, and he couldn't help but notice me.

'Don't take off your coat mate. You're on your way to the desert.'

If anyone else had said that to me I probably would have laughed in their face, but not PJ. I knew he meant every word, so I picked up my overnight bag (a reporter's only tool) and walked straight out of the office again. 'Ring me when you get to the airport,' added PJ as usual.

I was as happy as a pig in shit as I drove at high speed to Gatwick. At the airport, PJ was brief and to the point. 'The next flight to Algiers leaves in twenty minutes. You've got plenty of time, mate.' I made it by the skin of my teeth.

Once on my British Caledonian Trident, I felt as unrelaxed as

I always do on an aeroplane. There was no turning back now, though. I was on my way to North Africa for the first time since I'd had a nightmare time hitching round Morocco as a teen-ager. In those days you didn't dare talk to the locals in case they planted some dope in your pocket and then told the local constabulary.

I sat in my seat quietly contemplating the fact that there was no way I would be the first journalist on the scene. I knew that most of the daily newspapers had sent people out in the early hours. The only chance of success I had was if they didn't find Mark until Saturday, two days away, because that would give me a story for the *Sunday Mirror* that hadn't been in a daily.

I knew I wasn't exactly on to a winner, but it was always worth dreaming a little in this game.

Those dreams of a scoop were soon shattered when a finger tapped me on the shoulder and a familiar voice said: 'I can't imagine where you're going old chap.' It was an old foe from another downmarket tabloid. He was someone I wouldn't even have said hello to if I'd bumped into him in Fleet Street, but here, 30,000 feet above the Med, I could hardly avoid him. That's one of the unsettling things about the tabloids. You can be thrown together with a load of other hacks for a week or two of intense activity in some faraway paradise and then not even acknowledge their presence in a pub just seven days later.

'Most of them are already there, old son,' continued my irritating fellow journalist. I had forgotten what a boring pain in the arse this bloke was. 'I don't know why you Sunday boys are even bothering to come out. It'll all be over by the end of today.'

With those optimistic words ringing in my ears, I buried myself in a paper and tried to ignore the old hack for the rest of the flight.

On touch-down at Algiers, I felt a familiar sense of relief at having survived another flight – well, half-relief anyway. I knew I had to catch a plane home some time, so my self-inflicted torture wasn't over yet. At the terminal I just couldn't shake off my fellow hack, so in the end I gave up and we both headed off in the direction of a car-hire office inside the dour building. My departure had been so sudden I hadn't got to study a map of the country – all I knew was that we had to get to somewhere with a name that sounded like Taramasalata.

'You want to drive there?' asked the hire-car man incredulously.

'Yes. Is there a problem?' I asked, thinking that maybe his English was not so good.

Then I found out what the problem was. Taramasalata (the whole of Fleet Street later adopted this nickname) was in southern Algeria. And southern Algeria was further away from Algiers than London. In other words, we had so far managed less than half our actual journey. I didn't really fancy driving two thousand miles – in any case I'd be unlikely to get there until after the *Sunday Mirror* published. It was quite a blow to the morale at such an early stage in our desert adventure. I then discovered there was an internal flight down to Taramasalata, but I'd missed it.

Slightly lost for words at this juncture, I headed for the nearest phone. It was time to make one of my habitual 'I don't know what to do next' calls to PJ. Quite frankly, by the time I got through fifteen minutes later, I wished I hadn't. PJ kept me hanging on for ages after I'd got through to the newsdesk secretary. I couldn't understand it. Here I was, thousands of miles from home, and all I could hear was someone being given a bollocking about their expenses back in London. To make matters worse, the call was costing about a fiver a minute. I made a mental note not to forget that when I did my expenses for the trip. Sadly reverse-charge facilities were not available in little old Algiers.

Five minutes later PJ finally came to the phone. 'Sorry about that, cheeky sod thought he could get away with a meal in Claridges. What's up, mate?' he asked. It was fairly obvious he'd forgotten where he'd sent me. Not an unusual occurrence for a news editor when you have thirty or forty reporters wandering around the world on various assignments. But I had been the only one in the office earlier that day when PJ had sent me off to the airport. The least I could expect was that he would remember where I was.

'PJ, I am in – '

'Bloody hell. You're in the desert,' exclaimed PJ.

I didn't want to shatter his illusions at that early stage so I said nothing about it being another two thousand miles away.

'They've found him, mate. I should never have sent you,' he added.

I couldn't believe my ears. I've come all this way only to be told that Mark Thatcher has been found.

'He wasn't even badly hurt. What a pain, eh?' said PJ cheerfully.

'Well, what the fuck do I do now, PJ?'

PJ (ever the optimist) replied: 'Start digging, mate. You'll find something.'

I then decided to point out to PJ that I wasn't even half way through my journey to the desert. He wasn't impressed. But what came next really blew the wind out of my sails.

'I wouldn't bother wasting any money going right down to the desert, Wense. See what you can find in Algiers.'

So, the whole job was an almighty cock-up, but I may as well hang on in Algiers just in case Mark dropped in on his way home. Clearly he still hadn't understood how far I was from the action. Still, there was no point in arguing.

That Thursday night was rather muted to say the least. By this time the desert unit of pressmen had returned to civilization, leaving just a hardcore handful to follow Mark and his buxom blonde co-driver, along with a few diplomats trying to sort the whole fiasco out.

I was pissed off. I wanted a story, but the story, to all intents and purposes, was over. I retired early to my room and left the rest of the hacks knocking back water (the whole country was teetotal) and suffering from alcohol withdrawal symptoms. The air conditioning system in my bedroom was incredibly noisy and didn't seem to work properly. So what's new?

Next day was just as bad. Myself and a few fellow journos found ourselves wandering around the crowded streets looking in Marxist bookshops. Algiers is littered with them, and precious little else. After a while, I resolved to make a token effort to find out what was happening to our hapless hero Mark, who was still down south. I travelled to the British Embassy after phoning the ambassador Mr Ben Strachan and asking for an interview. I knew he had just returned from the desert saga, and I'd heard a rumour that Mark's dad Denis was flying down to pour oil on troubled waters. The British Embassy in Algiers – in common with many round the world – was like a home from home – a little piece of England in the middle of a teeming mass of Arab hustlers. Upon entry into the impressive looking Victorian building, I was shown to the drawing room (naturally) and offered tea and cucumber sandwiches (also naturally) while I awaited Mr Ambassador.

I had to pinch myself to make sure I wasn't dreaming all this. It was like a scene out of Oscar Wilde. Then mine host appeared, dressed (naturally, yet again) in an off-white cotton safari suit. He was absolutely charming, insisting on pouring me another cup of Earl Grey (naturally) and then proceeding to tell me all about his own adventures in the desert as part of the Mark Thatcher rescue team.

The problem was that he had given all this to the daily papers already, and I knew it. I was scratching for a story here, and it just wasn't forthcoming. We sat and chatted for about thirty minutes and the only reasonable line was that after Mark was discovered safe and well (the whole fuss had been caused by a mechanical fault in the car) Mr Thatcher told his son there was no way he could continue in the rally. "Not bloody likely" was the phrase Mr Thatcher used,' said Mr Strachan in fine old Etonian tones. So what, I thought to myself. It sounded like a good quote to tag on the end of a good story – but I didn't have a story to attach it to.

That afternoon I went back to my hotel in a dreadful mood. Even though it wasn't my fault, I felt as if I had somehow failed. In my room I got out my notebook and flicked through the few notes I had taken and, as is often the case, I found one line I had not pursued. I had the number of the hotel where Mark, Denis and the rest of the entourage were staying. I rang through and asked to speak to Mark's French co-driver.

My luck was in and so was she. Five minutes later I put the phone down after a brilliant if brief interview in which she'd revealed the most marvellous line of all – that when they found themselves stranded in the desert, hundreds of miles from civilisation, Mark had been in a right state. Apparently he told her to begin with not to worry as he was Mrs Thatcher's son and rescue teams would be dispatched within hours to find them. But as the hours went by, she said Mark became more and more distraught. I was over the moon and decided to write the piece there and then.

Within an hour I was on the phone to PJ. He was delighted and put me straight over to the *Mirror* copytakers to whom I dictated my great coup. Even the copytaker – a lady I recall – thought it was a great story. Normally they say nothing but a lethargic 'Carry on' after each sentence – being a copytaker is not the most exciting job in the world. After finishing filing the copy, I would have gone down to the bar to celebrate if they'd served alcohol, but since they didn't there seemed little point. Also, most of the journos had flown home by this stage, and there were only myself and a hack from the *Observer* of all places left. So instead I lay on the bed and imagined the sort of projection my story would get and how I longed for a pint of beer or a soggy bacon sandwich from the *Mirror* canteen.

I was about to drop off to sleep at about midnight when the phone rang. It was PJ. 'Well done, mate. Great story. The Editor is delighted.'

It all sounded familiar enough, but it wasn't being delivered in the ecstatic tones normally associated with PJ. I waited patiently for the punchline.

'But there's a problem. We can't run it.'

I was stunned – I knew the story was classic tabloid material and couldn't understand why it should be spiked. PJ explained.

Six weeks earlier he had dispatched a reporter to Poland at the height of the Solidarity uprising. That in itself might not seem so surprising, but the way the reporter gained entry to

Poland created a storm. Most journalists had tried and failed to get visas to visit the trouble-torn country, but *Sunday Mirror* man Greg Miskiw did not even try. Instead, PJ sent him in on a Vienna to Warsaw express train and, though it certainly wasn't PJ's idea, he ended up being disguised as a mailbag. It was a madcap scheme, as brave as it was crazy, and quite frankly it was doomed from the start. The main problem – besides breathing, eating and sleeping in a postbag – was that Greg was Ukrainian – a race of people not noted for their friendliness towards Poles, and vice versa. On arrival at Warsaw railway station, Greg emerged from his mailbag and strolled down the road to the nearest western-style luxury hotel (there actually were a few in Warsaw) and, when he couldn't provide a visa for the receptionist, was promptly arrested for spying.

Greg was slung in jail, and all our rival papers, sensing a classic dog-eat-dog story in the making, set their hounds a-sniffing to find out how this fiasco was ever allowed to happen in the first place. The *Sunday Mirror* went into severe panic stations. For the following five weeks, P.J. Wilson and editor Bob Edwards made regular trips to the Polish Embassy in London, spoke to prominent Eastern European politicians and sent letters galore pleading Greg's innocence and asking for his release. But it was all to no avail until Bob Edwards made a personal approach to Mrs Thatcher's office. That was on the Friday I was in deepest Algiers.

It seems that Mrs T's mob gave Edwards an assurance that she would seek Greg's release. Our revered Editor then returned to the office and immediately killed off my story about her son's disaster in the desert. He rightly believed that a reporter's life was more valuable than a story about Mrs Thatcher's son.

The whole situation was a godsend for Mrs Thatcher – another in a string of fortunate coincidences that have given her a reputation as one of the luckiest politicians around. Up until that point there was little any of her many publicity advisers could do to control press coverage of the story, and her opponents must have been rubbing their hands with glee as the details emerged. It was a far cry from the kind of publicity she was used to: a cosy fireside chat with a serious political correspondent, followed by a friendly handshake at the door of Number Ten and a brief wave to the waiting cameramen. Every interview was, in any case, a set-up job. If a journalist wanted to talk to her, a list of questions had to be submitted to her press team so that they could be vetted. Often certain questions would be returned with a terse note from the PM's cronies saying they were far too personal or sensitive for her to answer. Any hack who dared venture away from the pre-agreed list of questions would be swiftly shown the door.

But the Mark Thatcher story was out of her control – until the *Sunday Mirror* fell conveniently into her lap. The paper was, broadly speaking, supposed to be aligned with the Labour Party, and so was one of the few tabloids that might have been expected to make as much capital as possible out of her embarrassment. But there was no way it could do so and still expect her help in getting their man out of Poland.

'I'm afraid there's nothing I can do. My hands are tied,' said PJ, after explaining the whole infuriating scenario to me. 'Now, tell me about that line you mentioned earlier – Mark being banned from carrying on in the rally by his dad. That sounded harmless enough. Why don't you file that in the morning?'

So the next morning, drained and demoralised, I phoned over a story about Mark Thatcher being bollocked by Denis. It wasn't a bad tale, but it really didn't compare to the co-driver's revelation. I sounded so unenthusiastic about the story that the copytaker in London asked me if a close relative had just died.

'They might as well have,' I replied crossly.

Back in England, Mark was escorted by Denis straight to the PM's country seat at Chequers. Mark held his head high as he posed for sugary sweet pictures with Mummy and Daddy on the lawns of the imposing house.

It must have been a nice feeling for Maggie to get her boy back. Not only was he alive and kicking, but now she had him within her sights. No more deserts, no more escapades.

FIVE
The Odd Couple

TABLOID NEWSPAPERS HAVE ALWAYS BEEN OBSESSED BY
so called 'freaks' – anyone from Siamese twins to sex-change
policemen. The good old British public seem to have an
indefatigable fascination for people who are in any way out of
the ordinary, and the tabloids respond by providing a constant
diet of freak stories. P.J. Wilson was very much of the opinion
that the private lives of such people made great reading, so was
often sending reporters on extraordinary chases across Britain
in pursuit of weird and wonderful people. They could come
from all walks of life – politicians, millionaires, road sweeps.
They all have their fair share of oddballs in the family.

My most memorable brush with this style of journalism
began in downtown Birmingham, where PJ had flown for
lunch with the News Editor of the local evening paper in the
city. They were good mates and the local man often gave us
some first-rate tip-offs. PJ would think nothing of spending
about £300 on the round trip (including lunch), safe in the
knowledge that this particular contact would always provide us
with some great yarns. So it was not unexpected to see PJ
returning to the office at about five in very good spirits after his
extravagant double shuttle trip. This time he'd picked up a
story which sounded too good to be true. PJ made a habit of
digging up situations which sounded highly unlikely even by
tabloid standards, but this one made even the current output of
the notorious *Sunday Sport* look tame. Apparently a couple
had got married, had a child and then both changed sex. That
meant Mummy became Daddy and, you've guessed it, Daddy
became Mummy in front of the youngster's very own eyes.

I was completely astonished after PJ had sat me down and
given me the lowdown on this incredible tale. It's not often a

reporter is lost for words when briefed on a story, but I really couldn't believe that such a thing would happen.

But PJ was convinced it was true. The only reason the story had leaked out was because the couple had applied to change their Christian names on their social security claim forms. There was one big problem. No one knew those names. The informant from the social security offices in Brummie had refused to reveal them. Although I had the scent of a classic tabloid story, I was apprehensive about drawing a blank as, just half an hour after PJ had returned from his lunch, I found myself driving up the motorway in pursuit of 'the Odd Couple'. We had already decided what to dub them. On that drizzly Tuesday afternoon it really did seem like mission impossible: no names, no addresses even – just the knowledge that they lived in Handsworth – an area about the same size as Kensington and Chelsea. It was not going to be an easy task.

But the News Editor of the local evening paper was bending over backwards to help me in the search. No doubt the promise of much loot from PJ had something to do with that. He even specially laid on two reporters from the paper to help me scour the grotty city landscape looking for the sex-change couple. At first it really did seem to be a fruitless task. No one appeared to know them, and we could have been looking in completely the wrong area of Handsworth for all I knew. For three days, my team and I slogged around the streets looking for a Mrs who'd become a Mr and a Mr who'd become a Mrs.

Meanwhile, word had got out that the *Sunday Mirror* had mounted a large search party for the Odd Couple and by Friday other journalists, mainly from other Birmingham papers plus the *News of the World*, were also combing through Handsworth. Fortunately none of them appeared to be having any more luck than I was.

By Saturday morning I had got pretty fed up with ringing in to PJ and hearing him reply chirpily: 'Happy hunting mate. You'll find them in the end.' Did he have sixth sense, or was I just being plain defeatist, I asked myself. Time was fast running out if I was to meet the deadline for the following day's paper. It was eleven in the morning and I was no closer to locating them than I had been four days earlier. At this point a rather irritating mob from another local rag had decided to shadow my every move in the hope I would lead them to our quarry. Every shop I went into they followed minutes afterwards. It was becoming bloody annoying.

Eventually I decided on a sort of truce, and suggested to the rather rotund Brummie girl leading their pack that she should help rather than hinder our search. I took over her troops and we split up all the houses and shops in the area between us. We began a mass door-knocking session, which I had decided would last until midday. After that I was going to call it a day. By eleven-thirty we were as frustrated as ever – still getting nowhere fast.

Then I walked into a tobacconist's on a messy looking council estate. I wanted to buy some cigarettes and, as an after-thought, I asked the Indian gentleman behind the counter if he had ever seen the objects of my immediate desire.

He knew them instantly . . . I couldn't believe my luck. Was he sure it was the same people? Why was I bothering to ask? There can't be many sex-swap parents wandering around Birmingham. I could hardly contain myself. He then threw in the actual address – in a street just opposite the shop. I walked out of the shop with a wide grin on my face. I was the cat that had got the cream.

'You look pleased with yourself. Have you scored?' asked my rotund lady hack friend.

'No,' I lied. 'I'm just looking forward to getting home.'

I then pulled out my map of the area, spread it on the bonnet of my car, and assembled the local-paper troops. It was as if we were about to embark on an army exercise. I started pointing at streets, where they should continue searching.

'You go there,' I barked at one young rookie. 'You there . . .' And so on.

'And I,' I said, pointing to the street I knew they lived in, 'will try this one.' There was no way I was going to let anyone steal what I thought of as my story. I couldn't possibly let these local chaps in on what was happening, since they all had Saturday afternoon editions and so could run the story before the *Sunday Mirror*.

I then walked straight off in the direction of the Odd Couple. It was a rather quiet tree-lined street filled with those highly unattractive thirties-type houses that you always find in Brighton and Hove, to name but a few places. At number 15, I stopped momentarily and then carried on walking. I wanted to be absolutely certain that none of my local-paper rivals were in sight. Then I turned and strolled back towards the house and walked up the path. Before doing so I once again checked that all the other scribes were well out of the way – they were.

It took quite a lot of ringing before the door was opened by an elderly woman who certainly didn't look as if she'd had a sex change. She was also too old to have a three-year-old child.

My heart sank. Maybe Mr Patel at the corner shop had got it all wrong. Perhaps he'd completely misunderstood what I was on about. He might have thought I said sex shop instead of sex swap, not that this looked much like a sex shop, either. All the same I decided to interrogate the old lady in my finest policeman-style brogue.

'I wonder if I could ask you some questions. Is there a couple with a small child – '

Before I'd had a chance to finish, the old lady was pointing upstairs.

'They live up there,' she said.

I was about to crack the big one at last. I'd spent four days and nights tramping round the streets of Handsworth trying to find this wretched couple and now they were just yards away.

As I walked up the worn carpeted stairs to a door that vaguely resembled an inner door to a flat, I was just praying they would be in. Before I'd even had a chance to knock, the door opened and my eyes beheld a very strange sight. This person was dressed in a red blouse with a pert, lamb-chop style collar and a midi-skirt complete with the obligatory accessory of that particular district, white stilettos.

'Yes. Can I help?' The voice was distinctly croaky. In slightly nervous tones, I explained who I was immediately. There was no point in pulling the policeman trick. I had to get this one in the bag – and quick. Basically I had about an hour and a half before my copy deadline for next day's paper. Incredibly, I was in immediately. A sense of achievement came over me – but there were a hell of a lot of problems ahead.

The first one was that while I was successfully gaining a perfectly legal entry for a change, my 'helpers' from the local papers had managed to gather precisely the same information from residents in the surrounding roads. It's not surprising, really. This couple must have caused quite a stir when they started to walk round town in each other's clothes!

No doubt furious at my deceit, the young hounds had charged round to number 15, determined to ruin my fun. The result was that about five of them had just appeared on the Odd Couple's doorstep. At that moment, the bell rang. I rushed down the stairs and just stopped the old girl (whom I later discovered was Mum to one of the couple) from answering the door. 'Don't worry, we've decided to ignore the bell. It's just some door-to-door salesmen,' I explained, completely unconvincingly. Luckily she had a glazed, slightly dense look on her face, which wasn't helped by her pebble spectacles. She probably still thought I was a policeman. The old girl instantly obeyed my order and we duly ignored the bell for at least three minutes until the pack of young hacks stopped ringing.

But when I looked through the net curtains of the upstairs front room, I could see that these local paper boys and girls were no fools. They had heeded one of the basic rules of the trade – if no one's in, wait till they come home. And that is exactly what they were doing – doorstepping. The minutes were ticking away and I had to get the interview done and organise photos. There was only an hour or so left. By this time I had been introduced to the other half – a Chinese-looking hunk of a woman turned man dressed impressively in jeans and Doctor Marten bovver boots – and their three-year-old daughter, who was happily playing with her parents and managing to get their brand new genders right!

The Odd Couple

Suddenly I heard the familiar voice of the girl reporter whom I'd recruited for my search party and then duly dumped along with the rest of them. 'We know you're in there. Let's have a chat with them?' she said hopefully.

This was all very disturbing. I was running out of time and there was no way my Odd Couple were going to be able to give a coherent interview with all this racket going on outside. I rang the office and got them to book a room at the Holiday Inn in Birmingham city centre. I told them to arrange for me to meet a photographer there and then wondered how the hell I was going to get out of this flat without my victims being interviewed and photographed by the mob of local hacks now lining the pathway.

These two may have swapped sex, but they had enough nous to understand exactly what was going on – and, incredibly, they seemed to be taking it completely in their stride. Only thirty minutes earlier I'd never met them in my life, and now I was about to turn their safe, if strange, little world upside down. Why did they let me in in the first place? The answer is that I told them I understood what a traumatic time they were going through and suggested their case could prove an encouragement to thousands of others caught in what the tabloids have since labelled 'gender crisis'.

But my next task was far more tricky than talking my way into the flat. I had to find a way of getting out of it in one piece. There's only one thing for it, I thought, I'll have to walk them out with blankets over their heads. To make matters worse, I'd left my car about a hundred yards up the road. So, myself and my two new friends (daughter was left behind with Granny) strolled out through the front door into a scene from a Klu Klux Klan meeting.

The Odd Couple were each covered by a blanket down to their waists. I had to hold them each by the hand and lead them down this rather dull little street followed by half-a-dozen screaming hacks, furious that I'd stitched them up (their words not mine, though I know how they felt). Fuck knows what the neighbours thought, but I guess they'd already got used to a few strange goings-on with the gender benders.

'You bastard. You promised to share this one,' yelled the female leader of the local pack. I ignored every word and just smiled gently. There was little else I could do in the circumstances. The amazing thing was that some months later I came across the same female hack and she was incredibly charming to me, despite my outrageous behaviour in Handsworth. In Fleet Street – like Wormwood Scrubs – there is definitely honour amongst thieves (sorry, I mean journalists), but that doesn't stop us treating each other pretty badly at times.

On one occasion I was dispatched by PJ to interview a Nottingham miner who had fallen in love and married an American millionairess after a holiday romance. By the time I got to the sleepy mining village where he lived in a one-up one-down (what else?) I found the *Star* had beaten me to it. They were already inside the house with chummy, in the process of signing him up for his exclusive story. Fat-cat wife was back in the States meanwhile, blissfully unaware of the fun and games that were going on in little old England. Left sitting like a couple of idiots outside his house, myself and the photographer decided there was only one thing for it. We would have to mount a spoiling operation – one of the more wickedly enjoyable tactics employed by roving reporters.

I decided to try and disable the *Star*'s staff car that was parked right outside the house. Armed with a matchstick, I walked casually up to the vehicle, then stooped to pretend to do up my shoelaces. At that point I stuck the matchstick in the tyre valve and heard the air hissing out. It seemed incredibly noisy, and I felt as if the whole road must have heard it. But no one stirred and I realised that I had got away with it. Our next move was to sit and wait in our car until the *Star* man and his 'buy-up' emerged from the house. It wasn't long before they came out and we both watched, unable to contain our laughter, as the car was driven off at high speed, only to grind to a halt fifty yards up the road because of the flat.

The next stage of the plan was to jump out and try and grab a few quotes from the miner – i.e. fire questions at him in the street and hope he would be daft enough to answer. As we walked towards the *Star* man and his captive, they spotted us, dived into the car and locked the doors. There followed a ridiculous scene during which we stood and tapped at the window of the car over and over again but got absolutely no response from the occupants. Goodness knows what passers-by must have thought. For almost half an hour we tried every trick in the book to get them to open the car. The miner was even forced to lie face down in the back seat to prevent any photos being taken of him. Eventually we walked back to our car, completely stymied by their lack of co-operation.

Fearful that we might try and snatch pictures when they got out to mend the flat, the *Star* man and his miner struggled off down the road in his Ford Cortina, flat tyre thumping, and we never got our man. So much for spoiling tactics . . .

Anyway, back in Handsworth I had a different sort of set of hurdles to leap with my sex-swap couple. It was a reversal of the Nottingham situation, and I prayed I wasn't working against someone who would stoop to letting tyres down. I saw no sign of a flat, however, as I wondered how to unlock the car without risking anything ghastly like a snatch picture from one of the assembled mob. I pulled the Odd Couple together, told them to hold each other's hands, then dived inside the car, unlocked the rear passenger door, rushed round and pushed the pair of them head first into the vehicle. Somehow they kept the blankets over their heads throughout.

Once in the car I screeched off in the direction of the Holiday Inn. But my angry young rivals hadn't given up yet. Two of them jumped in a car and gave chase. It must have been a bizarre scene because I wouldn't let the Odd Couple take off the blankets until I was sure no one could get a snap. Anyone passing my car would have seen a panic-stricken me with two blanketed figures sitting huddled up together in the back seat as pursuing reporters tried to open the door to my car each time our vehicles stopped at a set of traffic lights.

Then I remembered an old trick that sometimes came in

useful when being pursued by the enemy. At the next set of traffic lights, I jumped out of my car and ran back to the hacks in the vehicle behind. I leaned in through the driver's window and said, 'Come on chaps give me a break.' The two hacks smiled and said 'No way.' I smiled right back, reached in, grabbed the ignition keys and threw them into a drain in the gutter and ran like shit back to my car. The two idiots were left stranded at the traffic lights. The last I saw of them was one of the hacks trying to pull open the drain cover and screaming abuse in my direction. Luckily I never ran into those guys again.

I then continued towards our hoped-for refuge at the Holiday Inn. The receptionist couldn't believe her eyes or ears when I checked the Odd Couple in. Both of them looked so unconvincing – you just knew instantly that they were dressed in each other's clothes. I tried not to think about it but I just kept wondering to myself, what the fuck am I doing here?

It was a train of thought that was to return about every five minutes for the following sixteen hours.

On the way up in the lift the porter looked as if he thought I was about to indulge in a three-way sex orgy and he clearly didn't approve. By the time we got to the rooms, I had about half an hour left to interview them and file the copy. Then the phone rang. In my paranoid state, I thought the local boys had already traced us to the Holiday Inn, so I answered and put on a foreign accent. I needn't have bothered. It was the photographer from the *Sunday Mirror*. Pictures take longer than words to process and get in a newspaper so I had to let him come up and take his shots while I interviewed them.

Funnily enough the chat and pictures went easily and I filed my copy to a round of applause from P.J. Wilson in London. But my job was far from over. Sunday newspapers have about six editions through the night, and though I had managed to file my story in time for all our editions, anyone from rival tabloids interested in the story would carry on pursuing it until the final edition deadline at about midnight on Saturday evening.

It was half-past four in the afternoon and I was going to have to hang onto the Odd Couple for another eight hours. I would have been relatively safe it if hadn't been for all those local hacks I did the dirty on. I knew they were furious and would undoubtedly by now have contacted the Birmingham representatives on the *News of the World* and the *Sunday People*, our two deadly rivals. That meant I would have to stay glued to my new friends. I really couldn't even afford to leave them in their room alone in case some artful scribe turned up at the door. As we settled down to watch one of those incredibly inane Saturday afternoon quiz shows, the phone rang. I was feeling reasonably relaxed as I had managed to switch off to a certain degree. I should have known better.

'I hear you're staying there for the evening,' said a voice. It was the News Editor of the local evening paper, the man who'd tipped the story to us in the first place and whose reporters I had just left high and dry. 'Could we pop along and have a chat with them?'

'Sorry, mate. No way. You can have them tomorrow. Your next edition doesn't come out till Monday anyway.'

He was furious but I stuck to my guns. It turned out PJ had given him my number not knowing about the shenanigans I had practised earlier. Paranoia was setting in once more as I put the receiver down.

'Why don't we book out of here and go and have a meal in Stratford?' I told my Odd Couple. They looked amazed. We'd just booked in to a hundred-pound-a-night suite and here was I suggesting we check right out. But to their credit they didn't complain. I suppose it was all a bit of an adventure to them. Anyway, we gathered up our things and departed.

Even getting out of the Holiday Inn proved difficult. My paranoia level was at a premium and I was convinced that the enemy would be lurking in every corridor. I went ahead of them to make sure the coast was clear. I knew it would only be a matter of time before the local News Editor tipped everyone off that we were at the hotel. We had to get out in one piece. As we rushed through the reception area and down to the underground car park, I stared wildly at every innocent hotel guest as if every one was the devil himself come up from hell to snitch my story. Quite a few of them stared wildly back.

Meanwhile, PJ had sent another reporter up to Birmingham to help me out. Unfortunately, he hadn't told me of this development, and at this point nothing on earth would have prevented me disappearing into the depths of Warwickshire to flee the larcenous gang. And while I was taking off like Nigel Mansell down the thirty-mile road to Stratford, my assistant was coming up by train, expecting a quiet little evening in a luxury hotel.

As we hurtled through the streets of downtown Brummie, I really did begin to wonder if I'd done the right thing by knocking on that fateful door just a few hours earlier. My assistant must have been feeling much the same way about following me when he arrived at Birmingham station to be told by PJ, when he phoned in, to hop in a taxi and head off in the direction of Stratford. Fuck knows what Shakespeare would have made of all this.

Then a really unforeseeable thing happened. I had stopped at a fairly unfriendly looking steak house about fifteen miles outside Birmingham with the Odd Couple because Cathy (that's the boy turned girl) was feeling peckish and fancied a really good steak and chips. The looks we got as we walked into the restaurant were amazing. Within moments I had come to the conclusion it was easier to look at the floor than at the gasping expressions on the other customers' faces. Most of them were neatly dressed mums and dads with 2.2 children out for a weekend treat. I don't think they were expecting to meet a sex-swap couple and a seriously harassed Fleet Street hack in full flight. Anyway, with our triplicate orders of prawn cocktail, steak and chips and a bottle of the finest Blue Nun in place, I rang PJ to tell him that my assistant should meet us at the steak house. Back at the table, like the true gentleman I am, I struggled to make polite conversation with my two new friends. It's not easy concentrating on the weather and the state of British politics when you're sitting in a crowded restaurant with a couple like these two.

'Mr Clarkson. Phone call for Mr Clarkson.' I jumped up, relieved at an excuse to take two minutes respite from the somewhat sticky conversation. It must be PJ, I thought, as I grabbed the receiver. Unfortunately that was not the case. 'We know where you are and we'll get that interview if it's the last thing we do,' came the now familiar voice of the local News Editor. I was sent into a blind panic. They seemed to know our every move. Nowhere was safe from the pursuing hounds.

The Odd Couple were just about to tuck into their prawn cocktails when I screamed, 'Forget it! They're after us. We've got to go.' I flung a ten-pound note at the waiter and headed for the door, only to crash straight into my assistant, who'd just got out of a cab from Birmingham railway station.

'Bloody hell, am I glad to see you, mate,' I said.

Luckily PJ had sent up a seasoned old hand rather than a young rookie to help me out in my time of trouble. We all piled in the car and carried on our crazy journey to Stratford.

The journey was harrowing. Whenever a car followed us for more than half a mile, it became a suspect vehicle, and I spent more time looking in the rear-view mirror than at the road ahead. Anyone would think I'd just sprung the Kray twins from jail the way we were behaving. It was getting more and more ludicrous by the minute, but worse was about to follow.

'Ooh. Ooh. I'm in agony,' groaned Cathy, former builders' labourer and karate expert and now a happily married mother of one. 'My stomach's killing me and I haven't got any pills left.'

'Pills?' I asked, images of an as yet unrevealed drug addiction running through the battlefield of my mind.

'My hormone pills. I've run out of them. You've got to do something.'

Hang on a moment, I thought, if she doesn't take her hormone tablets then . . . 'I'll start to turn back into a fella!' Cathy must have been reading my mind. Was I imagining it, or had that voice already dropped a pitch? Maybe the gender transition process was already going into reverse.

Now when you've got a crisis, it is traditional for the star reporter (me) to get the lowly assistant to do the dirty work, and that was precisely what I was about to do.

'Where are the pills?' I asked, as I struggled to concentrate on the traffic careering towards us on the busy road.

Cathy replied: 'They're in the bathroom at home. I forgot to bring out the other bleeding bottle.'

'You'll have to grab a cab and go back to the flat,' I told my colleague.

He looked heartbroken, and I couldn't say I blamed him. But a reporter's got to do what a reporter's got to do. I stopped the car at a railway station and, with Cathy groaning in the back seat, I got out and said in a quiet voice so as not to offend the Odd Couple: 'For fuck's sake make sure you get those pills or else she'll end up turning back into a man.'

It was hardly a moment to cherish, but it did have its funny side. That was certainly the opinion of PJ when I rang the newsdesk in London to tell them of my latest dilemma. 'What,' shrieked PJ, laughing profusely. 'We don't want to end up paying for another sex-swap operation.'

He seemed to have no useful advice to offer, so I decided to carry on to a hotel I knew in Stratford and not even tell PJ where it was in case he blurted it out to the local News Editor again.

Once in the hotel it was like a repeat of the earlier Holiday Inn operation. But this time we were all much more tense and nervous – particularly because my assistant hadn't yet turned up with the hormone tablets.

Dinner was served in our suite and, looking at my companions, I decided there and then that whatever time we finished with them there was no way I would stay the night in the hotel. I was going to struggle back down the motorway to my own bed if it was the last thing I did. It was an optimistic thought in the circumstances. After all, there was still no sign of the tablets and

The Odd Couple

I was seriously considering hospitalisation for the former labourer because s/he was clearly suffering considerable pain. The other half, still dressed in jeans and bovver boots was, perhaps surprisingly, a much gentler person. A university graduate and former social worker, s/he was altogether much easier to deal with. In fact, I got rather worried at one stage in the evening because I was convinced s/he was giving me the come-on, something I could do with like a hole in the head. However, this was most likely a figment of my fevered and paranoid imagination. By eleven o'clock the tablets still hadn't turned up so I rang the office, only to discover that another drama was going on back at the Odd Couple's flat. The whole of Fleet Street had, it seemed, descended on the street and were waving notebooks at anyone who knew the Odd Couple. By the time my poor assistant turned up, he faced a titanic struggle to gain entry to the flat, even though Cathy had given him the keys to the house. His problems were compounded by the fact that the old mum looking after the child thought he was a burglar and almost called the police.

This was, of course, highly amusing to the assembled hacks, who may have failed to get the story but couldn't resist a laugh at his expense. Eventually, my man got in, rummaged through the bathroom and found the correct bottle of hormone tablets. But his problems weren't over by any means. The pack knew that he must be going off to meet me and the Odd Couple, so when he got back in his cab the whole entourage gave chase. For the second time in about eight hours, the tiny street was awoken from its permanent slumber by screeching tyres as our man was pursued through Handsworth.

One hour and five cabs later he turned up at the hotel in Stratford, and I have to say I was a very relieved man – though I don't doubt the waiting was worse for Cathy than for me. As my assistant walked into the hotel room, she pounced on him with desperation.

'You've saved my life,' she gasped.

It was now nearly midnight and this nightmare was almost at an end. I am not sure if it was worth it, but the headline in the

Dog Eat Dog

Sunday Mirror the next day said it all: AMAZING SEX SWAP CASE – EXCLUSIVE. THE ODD COUPLE. NOW HE'S MUM AND SHE'S DAD.

I slipped out of that hotel and left that very strange pair of lovebirds fast asleep after their exhausting foray into the world of tabloid exclusives.

SIX

The Buy-Up

NEWSPAPERS SELDOM PAY FOR THEIR STORIES IN advance. Sure, they might offer the odd £50 to someone for some information, but big money isn't generally paid before the article in question is published. The 'buy-up', as it is called, has provided more tabloid column inches than anything else. If the Editor believes someone's personal story will help increase circulation, huge amounts can be paid, especially if it means securing exclusive rights and so squeezing out the competition. In the early 1980s, Fleet Street was buy-up crazy. The competition between the *Sunday Mirror*, the *Sunday People* and the *News of the World* was ferocious to say the least. Whenever a major news story broke, representatives of all three papers would be vying for the big buy-up.

Certain reporters on the Sunday tabloids were famed for their buy-up abilities. Often I would end up sitting around a table with journalists from the *People* and the *News of the World* bidding for some inside story or another. As with any other auction, we were all in the business of trying to con each other into believing we didn't really care who got the buy-up in the end and didn't think it was worth that much – the idea was to nip in at the end with a much higher final offer than could have been guessed at. The most popular subjects for buy-ups were (in no particular order) randy vicars' wives, employees of the royal family (nowadays they're contracted not to talk), soccer stars' secret girlfriends, wife-swapping airline pilots, sexy gym mistresses and a host of other fascinating people. The buy-up was not a simple process. It often lasted days, sometimes even weeks, and would nearly always involve a whole team of reporters from the paper that had won the auction.

Even with an exclusive contract in the bag, subjects would sometimes accidentally blurt out some vital info to the competition. Our job was to ensure that the story was not only exclusive, but also worth every penny paid. This could mean hiding the victim in a hotel to keep him or her away from rival papers. Frequently, young freelance journalists would be brought in just to 'babysit' the punter while the star reporter enjoyed a tasty four-course meal in the restaurant downstairs.

It was at the height of that buy-up era that I got involved in a story that dominated the headlines back in September 1980.

It was a Friday morning and the front pages of all the tabloids were running a good old-fashioned story about a famous soccer star being caught snogging a housewife in the front of his Jag. The car was parked on the edge of a golf course in Nottingham in the early hours of the morning.

The story had leaked out after an embarrassing encounter with the woman's aggrieved husband. Police were called to the scene when the footballer spotted the poor man tapping on the car window to ask why a soccer superstud was trying to have it off with his wife. In the panic that followed, the footballer tried to get away and drove straight into a lamp-post. It was the sort of story the tabloids love.

The soccer star in question was Peter Shilton, who is still one of England's number one goalies ten years later. The housewife was a Mrs Tina Street, who just happened to be dancing the night away when Shilton pulled her in a local disco. The two lovebirds then set off in his flashy car for the golf course car park – and the rest, as they say, became history.

At that early stage in the proceedings, only the most basic of details had been reported in Friday morning's papers. Therefore it was hardly surprising when P.J. Wilson dispatched me to Nottingham to 'get a full confession from the bird', as he so delicately put it.

I sped up the M1, anxious to get to Mrs Street's home and offer to make her rich in return for the full story. It was a classic tale and I knew it would do me the world of good to get a result. But by the time I arrived outside the Street family's modest terraced home, the whole pack had been there for quite a while.

At first glance it seemed a bit of a hopeless assignment. At least thirty journalists had got to the house ahead of me and they still had the next day's dailies to print their stories in before my paper reached the streets on Sunday. However, that also meant time was running out for them, so I decided I'd stand back and let the other journalists grab a few words with our femme fatal Tina Street, before moving in myself for the full confession about exactly what Shilton did to her in that car. There was no way she'd tell a whole mob in the street outside her home, so I took a back seat for a few hours.

At about six in the evening, she emerged from the bleak, grey house and the pack swarmed around her. Up until this point no paper had actually spoken to her or Shilton about the events of the early hours of the previous morning, which was why we were all gathered there with tongues hanging out.

'What happened in the car, Mrs Street?' was the question that was repeated over and over again. 'Did he make love to you?' and 'Is it true he had his trousers round his ankles?' were some of the other little gems emerging from the gutter. It was a typical tabloid scene, especially when you consider that most of her neighbours were standing outside their front doors listening to every word.

She replied tersely: 'Nothing happened. I really don't want to talk to anyone. Now go away. Leave me alone.'

Her words were like music to my ears. She was giving nothing away and that meant there would be a lot of meat left for me to chew on if I could persuade her to talk.

But the doorstepping pack were being very persistent, and while Mrs Street stood in the road, trapped by the crowd of scribes, I decided to knock on the door of the house and see if there were any relatives at home. That may seem a pointless move, but I once persuaded a woman at the centre of a wife-swapping ring to co-operate with me by locating her teenage daughter and using all my persuasive powers to get the girl to talk her Mum into playing ball. People always take more notice of their relatives than of strangers who come knocking on their door.

The door was answered by an elderly lady I took to be Mrs Street's mother. Mums always rally round in times of need, and they are always, naturally, on the side of their loved ones.

'Terrible the way they're pestering your daughter, isn't it?' I sympathised. 'Personally, I would never do that sort of thing.' Then I slipped in the following: 'I wonder, could I come in for a moment?' Within thirty seconds I was being made a cup of tea by Mum and offering her all the moral support I could muster. The huge pack of scribes had hardly noticed me, as they were hard at work on poor Tina. Part one of my plan had worked like a dream.

Soon the pack waved goodbye to Tina and let her drive off in her Vauxhall Viva. They dispersed and wandered off in the direction of the nearest pub, completely unaware that I was inside becoming new best friend to the Street family. I sat patiently and chatted to Mum in the kitchen. She seemed genuinely relieved that any journalist could be so charming. I knew that she was the key to my success, and was really pouring on the slush. She told me that her Tina would be back in half an hour, after fetching the kids. I decided it was a good investment of my time to just hang on in there.

When Tina Street did eventually come back she got quite a shock when I opened the front door to her own house and greeted her.

'Who the hell are you?' she asked. I tried to explain, but my traditional charm routine seemed to fall on deaf ears. She had obviously had enough of being harassed for the day. Then in stepped Mum to my defence.

'I think you should talk to this man. Then it's all over and done with. They won't leave you alone till you talk to someone.'

I must say I'd primed Mum very well. At this point I managed to persuade Mrs Street into her front room, where I explained to her that the *Sunday Mirror* would be prepared to pay her a lot of money (I didn't actually specify how much – having been trained not to commit myself unless absolutely necessary). She seemed interested in the cash aspect, and I knew she was beginning to bite on the bait.

We were just discussing the finer aspects of the story, like how Shilton had removed his trousers in the driving seat of the Jag just before trying to have sex with her, when I noticed a figure lurking by the front window. It was an old foe from a daily paper who'd been missing from the earlier scrum. In a desperate attempt to attract her attention he began tapping on the window, but it was far too late. He'd missed his chance, and when he saw me relaxing in an armchair, he knew it. Just to make sure the point was rammed home, I gave him a friendly two-fingered gesture. That's how you treat your friends in Fleet Street.

This same guy and I had an extraordinary tussle a year later in a flat in Hamburg, when we were both covering a story about two British girls who hitched a ride on a yacht crossing the Atlantic. The German captain ended up falling over the side and the mate was locked in a cabin by the girls after they claimed both men tried to sexually molest them. These two girls then managed to coax the yacht into a tiny harbour in the West Indies, from where their horrific story emerged. My deadly rival and I happened to call at the home of the German captain's widow in Germany on the same day. Luckily, I got there first; but when he turned up he tried to snatch the family photo album, which I intended keeping for reproduction in the *Sunday Mirror*. Naturally I snatched back, and a full tug of war ensued. The grieving widow looked on in horror as torn photos of her dearly departed hubby started fluttering out of the album. Eventually I won this very undignified scrap and slammed the door in my rival's face. He was not a happy man. The following week I spotted him in a Fleet Street bar and we had a chat and a laugh about our escapade.

A really good tabloid man never bears a grudge, and the Shilton story showed why. The next day the paper he worked for had an interview with Mrs Street which, along with every other daily, quoted her as saying that nothing had happened with Shilton. Of course he never went near Mrs Street, but had got the quotes from one of his other daily newspaper colleagues. Friends like those are invaluable on Fleet Street.

Yours truly was by now slowly but surely extracting the real truth from the statuesque, rather attractive redhead. I was by no means out of the woods, though. I was pretty certain that word would have got around that I was about to sign up Tina Street, and that would mean a number of raids from fellow Sunday hacks anxious to nick my exclusive. These thoughts prompted me to persuade Tina that we should go to a hotel to keep 'out of the way of all the other papers'. I don't think there is another profession where you can meet an attractive woman and, within minutes, be asking her to go to a hotel with you for entirely honourable reasons.

Having said that, my request didn't go down too well. Maybe she thought I was suggesting something of a sexual nature.

'I don't want to go to some foul hotel,' she said dryly.

Tina just would not be persuaded. In the end we reached a far from perfect compromise. I agreed we could go to her best friend's home in another part of town as long as she promised not to answer the door herself. To most people that might sound perfectly reasonable, but I had already broken the first golden rule of buy-ups: take them to a place where no one can find them. If they're with friends or relatives, there is always the risk that someone will leak the location to a rival paper.

But I had no choice in this particular case. The main thing was to stick with our Tina come what may. So off we set in my rusty old Renault on a one-way drive to near disaster. I hated the idea of her staying at a friend's house. Friends can put doubts in punters' minds, unless you get to them first.

Her best friend was a charming bubbly blonde, who was entertaining to talk to after all the hard work I'd put in with Tina and Mum. Unfortunately for me, though, she was also a sharp and intelligent girl. She clearly knew a chance to make a bit of cash when it came her way, and that meant trouble.

Hiding out in this girl's tiny terraced home, I felt reasonably secure from the search-parties of hacks on the prowl round the streets of Nottingham. For the first half-hour all three of us sat like old friends and watched TV together. Then I decided it was time to get down to the subject at hand, i.e., money for them and an exclusive for me. I was very aware that I needed to avoid being nailed down by them as to how much the *Sunday Mirror* would pay, but at this point the bubbly blonde took on the role of Tina Street's agent. And she was no slouch at the job, either. She wasn't going to let her chum sign any deal 'until you put the money on the table'. Now that was a bit of a problem. Obviously I didn't have any money on me; besides which, I was reluctant to put anything in writing until I'd heard everything Tina had to say. I was in a tricky spot and I knew it.

After listening to me humming and hawing for a while, Tina's new agent announced: 'All right, I'll ring up this *Sunday People* bloke at his hotel and tell him to come over and make a bid.' She waved a scrap of paper with a phone number on it in my direction.

My heart sank. The *People* were in touch. But how? Then the blonde admitted she'd rung up that paper's London office before I'd arrived and they'd given her the reporter's number at his hotel.

'I knew you lot were all after our Tina. I wanted to see what the others had to offer.'

It was rapidly dawning on me that this girl might be better at this game than I was. To make matters worse, I now knew that it was only a matter of time before my rivals showed up.

'Now, how much are you going to pay for Tina's story? It's about time you told us.'

Christ! It was time I got an agent myself.

'Why don't we try and slip out for something to eat?' I suggested, in a feeble attempt to camouflage my helplessness. I was up against the ropes now, and they knew it.

'Don't worry,' said she brightly. 'We'll nail you down on money before the night is through.' She had that knowing look on her face, and it worried me.

My attempt to avoid the issue of money by changing the subject to food and how hungry they must all be hadn't exactly worked, but at least there was a general nod of approval at my suggestion to go out for a meal. The truth was that I was itching to get out of that house before any hacks turned up.

But as I opened the door I discovered it was already too late. The sneering smile of a *People* rival greeted me from across the road.

'Hello, old chap. Don't you think Tina would like a word with me?' he asked gleefully.

There's nothing quite like being a tabloid hack on the attack. When you are not in possession of the buy-up, you can get up to all sorts of mischief, and really upset the apple cart for the journalist who's having to defend his story. Until I persuaded Tina to sign a contract, I was very vulnerable, and I didn't have to be psychic to know that this hack was going to make the most of my discomfort.

As the *People* man crossed the road I slammed the door firmly shut. What the hell was I going to do? I turned to Mrs Street and her blonde agent and told them supper was off. We had a siege on our hands. I didn't exactly start putting barricades up but, knowing the skills of that particular *People* reporter very well, I felt I could have done with a couple of tanks and some air support.

The corner I was in was getting stickier and stickier. One way out of this mess was to sign whatever piece of paper the blonde wanted me to. It would be a rash thing to do, but the look on that hack's face made me feel rash.

Tina's agent kept shoving this scrap of paper with astronomical figures written on it under my nose and saying: 'Look, you either give us a proper contract or we'll do a deal with him.'

A few minutes later I was signing a scrap of paper promising Mrs Tina Street £10,000 whatever happened. I must have been as mad as a March hare, but I just couldn't bear the thought of losing the story.

Meanwhile, the *People* man had been joined by a local news agency bloke and a representative of the *News of the World*. They were taking it in turns to knock on the door, and Mrs Street was getting understandably jumpy. So was I for that matter. I'd signed the paper, but I knew the gang outside would soon start on their party tricks – and when that happens, anything goes.

Then something was pushed through the letterbox. Before I had a chance to jump up and see what it was, the blonde had rushed to the hall. By the time I got there, she was reading a scrap of notepaper avidly.

I didn't dare ask what was in it, but I was pretty sure it was from a rival hound resorting to spoiling tactics on my exclusive – the exclusive I'd just signed a ten-grand deal for when in fact it was worth about two grand at the most.

'This note says you're a notorious liar and cheat and you never pay the money you promise to pay for stories,' said my blonde friend.

'Oh dear. I've been found out,' I joked. That was a big mistake. Now they were well suspicious. Trying to save myself I prattled on: 'Don't be daft. They're just trying to spoil it for us. What they hope is that you'll open the front door and give them an interview which they'll end up paying less money than us for.'

The blonde looked unconvinced. Mrs Street looked fed up. 'I'm hungry and tired. Why can't we go out for dinner?' she complained.

There was no way we could set foot outside the house at that moment, but I was breaking every rule in the newspaper buy-up book. I was allowing the punters to get hungry and annoyed, and letting rival hacks get to them. It was bad news all round.

Another noise came from the letter box. This time I could hear it opening but there was no sound of a note dropping to the floor. Instead a voice yelled: 'Don't believe a word he's telling you, Tina. He'll con you rigid. Make sure you get everything in writing.'

The only factor in my favour was that the blonde had already forced me to sign the scrap of paper. Unfortunately, though, the hack shouting these slanderous things about me through a letterbox in a two-up two-down in Nottingham wasn't far off the truth. I had an awful reputation for promising people the earth and giving them sweet f.a. For the next hour I endured endless verbal abuse from my friends outside. Yet I knew full well that I would meet and greet all of them in the Wine Press in Fleet Street the following week and have a laugh about the whole episode.

But right then I felt like the loneliest man in the world. I had just signed ten grand away, and my old enemy paranoia was beginning to get the better of me. What would the Editor say? Supposing the story turned out to be completely untrue? It was getting late and our Tina hadn't really given me the story yet. I wanted to know the full works – how Shilton had met her in a nightclub, danced with her and told her she had beautiful eyes. Then how he offered her a lift home and instead headed for the secluded car park. How he started heavy petting her . . .

'Look, Tina, we really do have to run through some of the details now.'

She looked pained. She obviously thought she'd already earned the £10,000 just by being with me.

'But I don't want to talk about it now.'

'It's now or never, Tina,' I said in a threatening manner. I really had had enough.

Tina sighed. 'I suppose our petting was a form of foreplay, but he was very gentle . . . ' All the delightful details poured out from between her lips – about how he kissed her, undid her blouse and took his trousers down.

She told how her husband appeared on the scene. She'd left him at home looking after their three kids while she went out clubbing with friends. When he turned up, she explained, 'I said to Shilton "It's my husband." He thought I was joking at first. Then he saw my husband knocking on the window.'

So it went on. The only question I never managed to get answered was how hubby came to be driving round a deserted car park late at night when he was supposed to be looking after the three kids. He claimed afterwards he was worried about where his wife was, so he went out looking for her. It wasn't an entirely convincing answer.

By the time she had told me everything it was very late on

Friday night and I was feeling knackered. Mrs Street and her blonde friend wanted me to leave the house so they could get some peace and sleep. They had refused my countless offers of a hotel, even though the only ulterior motive behind my suggestion was that it would enable us all to get away from the gang, who were still camped outside.

'Look. You can go to your hotel. They won't get near us,' said the blonde. I knew from the tone in her voice that I had no choice in the matter.

Luckily, an element of trust had returned to my relationship with the women, and I felt reasonably sure they wouldn't open their door to the other journos. But all my professional instincts screamed that it would be suicide to leave them alone in the house. What on earth was I going to do?

The answer was grim. I opted to sleep the night in my car parked outside the house, along with the rest of the pack. It was the only way I could ensure that no one approached the women. It was one of the most uncomfortable, sleepless nights of my entire life. It is no easy matter trying to sleep in a car parked in a noisy street in downtown Nottingham, especially when you're surrounded by rival journalists, after your story.

For two hours I tossed and turned, unable to settle. Then I noticed a figure lurking near the car. He seemed to be looking in. I kept my eyes shut to see whether he had an interest in me or if he was just a car thief. He didn't hang around, but walked over towards the house. Suddenly, I realised what was going on. He was trying to make sure I was asleep before knocking Tina up. Cheeky bastard, I thought, as I jumped out of the car and yelled at him: 'Leave them alone, mate. They're mine.' It was the *News of the World* scribe. He looked well pissed off, but said nothing and skulked back to his vehicle. Shortly after this, the police arrived on the scene.

Quite understandably, the neighbours had become alarmed at the sight of three men asleep in parked cars in their street. It was hardly normal behaviour in a dull provincial suburb. In situations like this, the local constabulary are either incredibly helpful and sympathetic, or they are just plain nasty. Unfortunately on this occasion they were the latter. We were made to feel like scum, and I put my foot in it by saying I had an exclusive contract with the woman inside the house we were all camped outside.

The PC looked understandably confused. 'Well, why do you need to sleep outside their front door then?' he asked. Quite a reasonable question, really.

But none of us were going to budge. He tried to tell us we weren't allowed to sleep in our cars, but we all knew better. We were in a public place and there was nothing he could do about it. But that didn't make him any more sympathetic to our situation, and he parted with the reassuring advice that 'I'll nick the lot of you if you cause any kind of disturbance.' So nice to have the local bobby right behind you.

Meanwhile, the sleeping beauties slumbered on, blissfully unaware of the fracas going on outside.

At seven the next morning bleary-eyed from lack of sleep, I knocked on the door of the house, no one answered at first and I immediately became panic-stricken. Then a voice – I think it was the blonde – came from the hallway.

'Go away.'

'But it's me, Wensley.'

'I don't care. We don't want you in here.'

What was I going to do. I'd bought this woman up for the *Sunday Mirror* and now couldn't even get in to the house where she was staying. PJ would be furious, and I'd be the laughing stock of Fleet Street if this got out. I went back to my car feeling utterly dejected. Luckily the other hacks were still snoring away in their respective cars, oblivious to my plight. For thirty minutes I sat in my car not knowing what to do. Then I went back and gave it another try.

The blonde came to the door again. 'Look, I told you to go away,' she said.

'But we've got a deal' I pleaded. I was really suffering. 'What's going on. You can't do this to me.' Suddenly I realised I sounded more like a victim than a hack. It was awful.

'Tina is upset because you didn't take us out for a meal last night. You made a promise and you didn't keep to it.'

I couldn't believe what I was hearing. This whole assignment was in jeopardy because I hadn't taken a Nottingham housewife out for a slap-up meal.

'But we couldn't get out,' I moaned. Shit, I thought, this is getting silly. But it's funny how the simplest things upset people. I had to come up with a rescue plan to salvage the whole operation, which now appeared to hinge on Mrs Street's appetite.

'What's the best restaurant in Nottingham?' I asked.

Long silence followed by: 'Smiths. Why?'

'Well, that's where we're going to tonight.'

'All right, come in.'

The door was unlocked and, unspeakably relieved, I strolled in. I'd managed to avert disaster, but the way these two were behaving, I knew I needed to keep an eye on them until the first editions of all the papers dropped at 8.30 that evening. A slap-up meal would help ease the agony.

I settled in to the house, and blowed if they didn't get me some breakfast! I got the occasional glimpse of one of my rivals sitting in his car outside. It was really sweet to munch on my toast and watch them suffer outside.

That morning I broke yet another golden rule and telephoned over my story to London from inside the house with the women. This is a highly risky thing to do as most punters go a bit funny when they hear the way a journalist has written his or her copy. There is always a special emphasis on words and phrases that they thought weren't that important. And people always expect you to leave out the embarrassing bits of their stories, as if those aren't the very parts that make the public buy newspapers in the first place. Worst of all, people imagine that once their names are splashed all over a tabloid, they are finished, and their lives will never be the same again. As a result they often get last-minute jitters. But the truth is that today's news is forgotten by tomorrow.

Anyway, as I merrily filed away – 'Redhead Tina Street, the

wife found by her husband in England goalkeeper Peter Shilton's car, has decided to make a complete confession about the incident –' Mrs Street tried to interrupt me.

'Do you have to mention Shilton's name?' It was a naive question. After all, he was the whole point of the story.

'Of course I do, Tina. He's already been named in every national newspaper in the country, so what difference is it going to make?'

'But I'd rather keep him out of all this.'

I gave her the only possible reply: 'Look, Tina. You name Shilton or we forget the money.'

She said nothing and I just carried on filing my story to the *Sunday Mirror*. But more daft interruptions followed, and it soon became clear that Mrs Street really didn't have a clue about papers. If she had had her way, I would have written a story about a woman of no particular age being spotted by police in an un-named make of car in a car park with an un-named man. That wasn't going to work, and I think the message eventually got through. One hour later I managed to complete filing my story.

Just before lunchtime the three of us emerged to find no one outside. I was very surprised, and pleased that, hopefully, there would be no more dramatic upsets.

That afternoon was spent taking photographs of Mrs Street for the paper and buying her a whole new wardrobe, courtesy of the *Sunday Mirror*. The editor wanted her to look her best for the photos that would appear in the paper the next day. Tina was, needless to say, delighted with this opportunity to update her wardrobe for free.

We had a lot of time to waste before the first editions dropped and, quite frankly, I could sense that Tina and her blonde friend were getting sick of the sight of me. The feeling was mutual, I can assure you girls. But all this hanging around was part of the buy-up ritual. No tabloid could afford to release the subject of an exclusive deal until after the rival papers had come out on Saturday evening.

Tina and her friend got their slap-up meal in the end. But her fee – negotiated so professionally by the blonde – was lowered thanks to the intervention of a *Sunday Mirror* executive. He was dispatched by P.J. Wilson to Nottingham the following week to 'persuade' them to accept less money.

Meanwhile, I am happy to say that Tina needn't have worried: Mr Shilton's career and marriage have carried on completely unaffected to this day.

SEVEN
Make Your Excuses and Leave

THERE IS ONE PROFESSION THAT NEVER CEASES TO fascinate the great British Sunday tabloid public. Famous celebrities may come and go. Wife-swapping headmasters don't always make the grade. Footballers' love lives have a limited novelty value. But any story involving prostitution will run and run – especially if a few sordid details are regularly included. In fact, the more innuendo the better. People, quite simply, lap it up. There is nothing they like more than to read about the adventures of Madam Sin, Wendy Whiplash or Lesbo Linda.

Only recently, the ultimate prostitute story was exposed in the shape of stunning Indian-born Pamella Bordes. This dark-haired beauty had managed to lead an amazing 'double life'. She went out with newspaper editors (serious papers, of course) and politicians, but secretly worked as a high-class call girl. Her joint careers were coming along nicely until a *News of the World* reporter decided to book her services. The rest, as they say, is history.

Stories involving prostitutes come in all shapes and sizes. In the 60s and early 70s the *News of the World* cornered the market with an article every week on some massage parlour or other that offered 'extra services' to its clientele. When the *NoW* changed its format from broadsheet (about the same size as *The Times* is today) to tabloid, there was uproar. Journalists and readers feared that all those stories would die out because there wasn't enough room in a small newspaper to run all the sordid details that everyone so loved to read. At first their protests seemed well founded. Classic headlines like MASSAGE GIRL'S BROTHEL ON THE RATES! and WE EXPOSE NAUGHTY SCHOOLGIRL VICE RING were no longer appearing with such regularity.

But prostitution as a Sunday newspaper subject was far from dead. Instead, a more sophisticated version of all those old-fashioned exposés began to emerge. Instead of turning over small-time brothels which weren't really doing any harm – except to the bank balances of a lot of men – the *News of the World*, *Sunday People* and *Sunday Mirror* began to hunt down the more sophisticated practitioners of the world's oldest profession. They were known as call girls and, unlike their suburban counterparts, these girls didn't work out of dingy terraced houses, dodgy-looking massage parlours or just plain street corners. They were 'supplied' through expensive advertisements in a whole variety of glossy magazines.

These adverts would normally read something along these lines: 'Massage service. We will visit your hotel any time, day or night, for soothing relief. Ring Samantha on . . . ' The idea was that the magazine would think it was a legitimate massage service, while the reader would know otherwise. Strange logic, to say the least. But for many years these adverts flourished, untouched by the 'high moral standards' of publishers and police. Another thinly-veiled disguise for call-girl networks were adverts for 'Escorts. Attractive girls will accompany you during your stay in London . . . ' It was big business. The girls were usually 'run' by a madame or pimp who took all the calls in response to the ad and would then contact one of his or her girls and tell them to go to the punter's address. More often than not that punter would be a visitor to London staying in one of the big West End hotels.

I don't know if many of these men (and sometimes women) were ever naive enough to think they were ordering up a soothing massage or a platonic friend for the evening. But they'd soon get the message when the girl got to the hotel room. 'It's twenty-five pounds for the agency [pimp/madame] and extras will cost you from thirty pounds upwards. That's for hand relief, then there's French and the full works, which will cost you more.' Something along these lines was usually established within two minutes of the girl's arrival.

I am sure you can well imagine what happens after the vulgar subject of money has been settled, if you are a genuine punter. But as a journalist it is a very different cup of tea altogether. When hacks are turning over call girls they are supposed to get the offer (hand relief, French, and so on) recorded on tape and then make their excuses and leave. But it just isn't that easy to leave an often stunning looking bird lying flat on her back on a double bed with the feeble excuse that 'I've got a dreadful headache, love. Take this money and call it a day.' The Street of Shame is filled with survivors who've resisted the temptation, and a whole lot more who've invested their newspaper's cash in a bit of love-play. After all, if you're exposing a call-girl racket you're hardly going to order a girl using your real name and rank on the paper, so you're well protected from recriminations. When the girl arrives at your room, as far as she is concerned you are just another punter. So why not take advantage of the situation? It's a tricky dilemma, I can assure you. It's only the paranoid (like me) and the plain boring (like many on Fleet Street) who really do make their excuses and leave.

In the 1970s there were at least fifty such call-girl operations in London. Many of the women were making over £1,000 a week from wealthy tourists and businessmen. A successful call girl never had a problem walking straight to a room in any of the capital's top hotels because she would have had the doormen in her pocket. In other words, the hotel staff got backhanders for allowing the women free passage into these very plush establishments.

In recent years there has been a significant crackdown on this business, and I am reliably informed that there are fewer call girls touring the capital's best-known hotels than there were ten years ago. But, back in those days, lobbies and lifts were filled to the brim with surprisingly glamorous hookers who knew they could earn at least £250 a night if they managed two clients an evening. The staff of all three downmarket Sunday tabloids knew all about call girls and the way they operated. Therefore it was no surprise that P.J. Wilson spotted an opportunity to launch a decent(ish) exposé when he noticed that Saudi Arabia's King Khaled was in town with a vast entourage – most of whom were staying at one of the most exclusive hotels in London. The King himself plumped for the guest suite at Buckingham Palace.

In his own inimitable way, PJ had convinced himself 'that Khaled's entourage are sure to get up to some right mischief'. He was certain it was going to be the major story of that week – even though he was basing his expectations on pure guess-work. This wasn't going to be one of those half-hearted operations. He wanted me to lead a whole regiment of journalists into the West End of London to get the story. One of the golden rules of covering these vice sagas is that you must go equipped with as many reporters as possible. The more witnesses the better.

On a lovely sunny day in June 1981, I set off to suffer four days and nights in the sumptuous hotel where the Arab brigade were staying. My wife must have thought it most eccentric to have her husband spending the week in a luxury hotel turning over Arabs and prostitutes, especially as the hotel was only twenty minutes from my home.

My team of eight freelance hired hands were to meet me near the hotel later that evening. Not even the *Sunday Mirror* was going to pay for ten rooms at £100 per night on the basis of a News Editor's hunch. One motive behind P.J. Wilson's thoughts on the 'Sexy Nights' story was the way the Saudis had been treating some of our subjects living in their desert kingdom. There had been recent stories of Brits being flogged for petty offences and we both felt that some tit-for-tat revelations would be popular with our readers. On top of that, our story would prove that Arabs in London regularly ignored Islamic laws banning adultery, alcohol and gambling. As anyone who frequents London's hotels and casinos will know, we were on to a sure-fire winner there.

When I arrived at the hotel, the reception area was teeming with slightly dodgy looking Arab types wearing aviator-style sunglasses and white suits. A couple of them were even dressed in the traditional headgear as well. I didn't even know at this early stage if any of them were Saudis – but who cares! I booked in under a false name. PJ had already warned me the royal party would check out every person staying in the hotel and if they discovered a journalist was in their midst there would definitely be trouble. In any case, it added to the fun of the situation to use a fake name. Imaginatively, I chose 'Browne' – with an 'e' of course. PJ was also certain that the porters would be supplying the girls. He told me knowingly: 'They're all at it in those posh hotels, mate.' So, as I was going up in the lift with an elderly bellboy (in his sixties at least) I dropped a few subtle hints like: 'I'm over here on business. Where's the action?' And: 'Don't seem to be many pretty girls around . . . ' both comments got zilch response other than a 'heard it all before' look on his face. Still, I thought to myself as he deposited my overnight bag on the bed and waited for a tip, maybe he'd earmarked me as a potential punter and I'd get a call later.

The paper had assigned one other staffer to the job, and he had booked in to a room on the other side of the hotel. We'd arranged to meet in the bar (where else?) thirty minutes after check-in.

The bar turned out to be virtually empty except for him and me, plus two stunning blonde women dressed up to the nines. It was late afternoon, but these women looked as if they were about to attend a banquet with the Queen.

'Arabs love blondes. Do you think these two are on the game?' I muttered under my breath to my mate.

He looked unconvinced. But we stood there for twenty minutes sipping vodka and oranges, just watching their every move. God knows what they thought of us. I'm afraid we must have stuck out like a couple of sore thumbs. At one stage, I thought seriously about propositioning them to test the water and see if they were real pros. In fact, I had just got up to walk over to them to ask them their rates when two perfectly respectable looking businessmen-types walked in and greeted our 'upper-class tarts'. They looked suspiciously like their husbands. There we were, about to brand two civilized thirty-year-old blondes as Saudi Arabians' call girls, when in fact they'd probably just popped up to London from Cobham for a shopping trip.

Meanwhile our rendezvous with the eight freelancers on our team was fast approaching. We had arranged to assemble in a pub just around the corner from the hotel I knew would be much cheaper for rounds of drinks – and a bit more discreet.

When I walked into the pub and saw the assembled team, I knew I'd made a big mistake allowing PJ to choose them. Half of the eight were so young and inexperienced they wouldn't spot a prostitute if she was staring them in the face. The other four were slightly over the hill to say the least. There were a couple of experienced hands amongst them, but the sight of them all hunched apprehensively round a table didn't exactly fill me with confidence.

Exposing prostitutes is not as easy as it sounds. Earlier that same year I had been involved in an operation that might have been one of the biggest stories of the decade, but all ended in nothing. It all began when some bright spark on our newsdesk decided it would be marvellous if we investigated the 'business affairs' of a vice queen known as Madam Bleep. She was given this nickname when it was revealed in a court case that she used to give each of her prostitutes a British Telecom bleeper so they could be instantly alerted when a client called. Back in the early 1980s, a bleep was an unusual device for anyone to use, let alone a vice queen.

Anyway, the plan was to order as many prostitutes as possible at a variety of top London hotels and interview them about Madam Bleep. Armed with the relevant phone numbers from our crime specialist, who sensibly steered clear of actually working on the story, a team of six of us headed off into the night.

My brief was to base myself at one of the largest and best known hotels in the capital and start hitting those phones. Pretending to be a genuine punter, I had to order a girl by asking for a body massage. The woman on the other end of the line would then ask for my number and a girl would ring back.

It turned out to be first time lucky (or unlucky, depending on which way you look at it). Within minutes of my original call to the woman (probably Madam Bleep, although I didn't realise it at that time) another, younger female voice was on the line.

'Hello, my name is Cindy, I understand you want a massage at your hotel. The charges are twenty-five pounds for a massage and the price of a taxi there and back. Would you like any extras?'

That was what I wanted to hear. 'Yes, what do you have on offer?'

'Hand relief is thirty pounds, full is forty-five, and French fifty.'

'OK. I'll decide when you get here.' I volunteered keenly.

Thirty minutes later, there was a knock on my door.

I opened up and there was this rather ordinary woman attempting a charming smile.

'Hello, I am Cindy. What's your name?'

Naturally I replied 'John. John Smith.'

She was wearing riding boots, black trousers and a red blouse and looked more like a Surbiton housewife than a £100-a-night hooker.

'Now, what do you have in mind?'

At this point I needed to switch the conversation around to her and her employer Madam Bleep. There was only one thing for it.

'Look, I know this might sound strange, but I'd really like to talk for a bit first.'

'Sure, you want to talk dirty before you fuck me?'

'Well, no, that's not exactly what I had in mind actually. I just wanted to talk to you.'

'OK. But it'll still cost you thirty pounds for fifteen minutes.'

Most people talk for free, but with this lady time was money.

We got talking and she spilled the beans all about Madam Bleep's little vice operation, and even proudly showed me her bleep, which she kept in her handbag. I never told her I was a reporter, but she turned up the TV really loud before incriminating herself in any way. It must have been fairly obvious that I wasn't an ordinary punter, so just to cover herself she made sure that any tape recording would be drowned out by the sound of the TV. The money clock was ticking away and I already owed her £120 by the time she got to the interesting bits – some of her other clients. The one thing I've learnt about call girls is that they rarely bother lying if they are talking to a client. They work on the basis that he's not going to land them in the shit because he shouldn't have been with her in the first place. This particular woman had some fascinating clients, as it turned out, and she was positively proud of them.

In graphic detail she told me how one showbiz personality, renowned for being about as straight and true as they come, used to call her up regularly for a 'complete night of the works'. The 'works' meant being beaten black and blue by this woman and then being humiliated in every way possible.

'I couldn't keep a straight face when I looked at him on the telly the other night. If only his fans knew,' she told me.

Apparently his favourite trick was to make the girl put a dog collar and lead around his neck and then ride him all around the room, kicking and scratching him and calling him every obscenity known to mankind.

'He really liked me to humiliate 'im. I thought it was a right laugh,' explained Cindy, thoughtfully.

But her other celebrity client was even more outrageous. His TV show was watched by millions. Even the Royal Family were said to watch his show. Goodness knows what they would have said if they'd known what he got up to every now and then in a West End hotel.

Cindy sat, completely straight-faced at the end of one of the twin beds, sipping coffee as she revealed: 'He used to eat my knickers.'

'What?' I said incredulously.

'He liked eating my knickers.'

I started laughing. This really was the ultimate. TOP TV COMIC EATS WOMEN'S PANTIES – SHOCK HORROR. I could see the headlines there and then. It turned out, according to Cindy, that this guy liked to make her rub them in his face and then push the entire garment in his mouth before 'he sucked all the juices out'.

It sounded pretty foul, but this knowledge certainly improved his TV performance from then on, as far as I was concerned.

Within seconds of this last revelation, I had made all the excuses I could think of and got Cindy out of my hotel room so as to ring the newsdesk with the incredible story of the knicker-eating comedian.

'Not a chance, mate. We'll never prove it. What on earth are you going to do to stand this one up? You can hardly go knocking on his door and asking him if it is true he likes eating prostitutes' knickers, can you?' My boss had a point.

'Even if you did ask him, he'd have a lawyer's letter round to her place in no time, threatening legal action if she continued repeating those allegations. Then he'd be on to us and it'd be his word against your report of the words of a common tart.'

It's always the same with prostitutes. Even if you can get them to court, they don't make good witnesses.

Back on the 'Sexy Nights' story, having surveyed my ragged troops I decided it was time for action. My briefing was simple. I wanted them all to find vantage points inside the huge reception area of the hotel and sit and read a paper or something and just watch everyone who came in and out of the hotel. If they spotted an obvious tart, then they were to wait until the girl left the hotel, then follow her and try to get an interview.

'You'll know if she's been with the Khaled mob because they've taken over the entire eighth and ninth floors,' I said helpfully. 'All you've got to do is watch where the lift stops after they get in.'

It sounded straightforward enough.

Unfortunately, that's not how it turned out . . .

The hacks left the pub in groups of two, walked round the block a few times, then drifted into the hotel in dribs and drabs – and dribs and drabs is what they looked like. My staff colleague – Greg Miskiw, he of the Polish escapade – and I returned to our rooms to give the mini-army time to get settled in the hotel lobby.

When we sauntered into the reception area it was like a scene from an Ealing comedy. Our crack team were dotted around the lobby reading copies of the *Evening Standard* and sipping double scotches. The cheeky buggers knew they could claim what they liked on expenses for this particular mission. (Mind you, I am hardly one to talk.) This was all very well, but there were hardly any people in the reception area apart from eight blokes dressed in macintoshes, with their top buttons undone and ties loosened. Greg and I had great difficulty containing ourselves. It was such a ludicrous sight. But the operation was under way and we had to just plough on and hope for the best.

It was still early days, about eight in the evening to be precise, so the two of us left our troops in the thick of the action and retired gracefully to the bar to consider the dinner menu. It was our prerogative as staff reporters on the paper to enjoy a decent meal while the freelancers in the lobby carried on their 'secret' observation programme. They could always eat much later in the local café, I commented thoughtfully to Greg.

It was ten by the time we'd finished our four-star dinner and I turned to Greg and said 'Maybe we should pop out and see how the boys are getting on?'

We wandered out of the restaurant and into a sea of inactivity. Of the eight who had originally sat down hours earlier, only six seemed to be present. Maybe two of them have chased after prostitutes who've left the hotel, I hoped. And one of those seated had actually managed to fall asleep behind his copy of the *Evening Standard*. I walked quietly over to his chair and gave his shin a huge whack with my brogues. He awoke with the words: 'Not a sausage has happened. No girls, nothing.' I was trying to look as if I wasn't actually talking to him. I didn't want anyone in the hotel working out what was going on if, by any chance, they hadn't already done so.

I muttered: out of the side of my mouth: 'Well then, where are the other two.'

Sleeping Beauty answered: 'They've been kicked out by the manager because they only bought one drink each all night.'

Bloody marvellous. One quarter of my observation team has pulled out because they were too mean to buy a drink. I suppose they thought they couldn't get away with claiming for drinks all night on their expenses. Mind you, at least they would be sober. It was more than I could say for the remainder of my platoon. They had been so diligent at ordering drinks to avoid being sussed that now they were totally pissed. This assignment so far had all the hallmarks of a fiasco, and I knew it.

Still, we had a job to do and I knew that the peak time for prostitutes was fast approaching. Suddenly two incredibly brassy looking women came waltzing through the hotel's roundabout doors. They were laughing and giggling loudly to each other. One was a striking blonde in red-leather trousers. The other a brunette in black leather skirt, black stockings (they may well have been tights but stockings sounds better) and stilettos (get the message?).

'Fuck. That's got to be two of them,' I muttered to Greg as we walked away from our men in case anyone spotted me talking to them. I turned back to see our 'undercover' operatives all watching the girls avidly as they pranced into the lift without even bothering to go to the check-in desk. That was an absolute giveaway – only a tart would ignore reception and go straight up to the rooms. They would already know the room number, and would want to attract as little attention as possible. The irony of that is that they were so outrageously dressed that you could not help but notice them. Anyway, these two were as bold as brass. They were no doubt looking forward to a cash (and many other things) in hand situation.

Eight pairs of eyes studied the lift indicator light as it went up to floor nine and stopped. We knew we were in business. They had gone to see our Saudi Arabian friends.

The following thirty minutes were eccentric to say the least. Every time the lift came down and the doors opened, all eyes turned to stare at the people getting out. It must have been pretty unnerving to be eyeballed by a brigade of pissed raincoats. But there was no sign of the girls. Maybe they weren't hookers after all. Perhaps they were wives or relatives? Hang on, they wouldn't be dressed in leather and stilettos, would they? At one stage I began to think that perhaps the women had put on different disguises to slip out of the hotel unnoticed. It was silly to even consider it, but when you're bored and hanging around a hotel lobby waiting to talk to prostitutes, it's hard to keep your mind on the straight and narrow. At this point I was standing near Sleeping Beauty, who at least hadn't fallen asleep again. We both watched again as the lift light went up the floors and stopped at the ninth. Maybe we were in luck at last. It seemed to stop at that floor for ages before starting its descent. At this stage, all we had to go on was a light, nothing more. Yet, I was certain this was going to be our girls on their way out of the Saudi boudoir. The bloody lift kept stopping at different floors on its way down, which was going to make it difficult for us because it meant a lot of people were going to emerge from the lift when it finally arrived. The doors cranked open and out walked an old lady and her Yorkshire terrier.

I was convinced there was something fishy going on. Maybe the girls had got out of the lift on the first floor and slipped out by a service stairs? I was just about to go and check the rear of the hotel when our girls surprised the lot of us by waltzing out of the lift while we were still all gaping at the old lady with the Yorkshire terrier. They looked pretty pleased with themselves.

I kicked Sleeping Beauty and barked at him: 'Follow those girls and talk to them.'

He jumped up, a dishevelled character at the best of times but a lovely guy all the same, and cantered after the two girls who were flush with money and other things besides. They walked through the roundabout doors and turned left. My man, who you must remember had drunk about eight double scotches by this stage, blasted through those doors at a furious pace.

The problem was he went so fast that he ended up exactly where he started – back in the hotel lobby. It really was Keystone Cops time! The problem with roundabout doors is that if you push them too hard you can't get out of them until they slow down. Sleeping Beauty had just discovered that fact, and it had cost us a vital interview with two hookers who'd just spent half-an-hour with King Khaled's men – the very thing the *Sunday Mirror* had spent thousands setting up.

I was fuming but the rest of my unit were laughing their heads off. On reflection, it was a hilarious scene because Sleeping Beauty just didn't know where he was for a few seconds after he arrived back in the reception area, and stood there blinking like Bambi in a forest fire. I was still angry and muttered under my breath to him: 'Just sod off home, mate.'

All in all it was a disastrous night's work. The ultimate touch of farce was provided by our one and only photographer, a sweet old boy in his seventies, who had decided in his wisdom to stand directly outside the hotel with three cameras round his neck. He looked as if he'd just arrived at Wembley Stadium for the cup final. As you can imagine, not many prostitutes tend to stop and pose for photographs on leaving a hotel. But the old snapper just couldn't understand why he needed to keep his cameras hidden from view. Still, it didn't really matter, since the whole evening had degenerated into a monumental cock-up. At about two I retired to my luxury suite and decided that a totally different approach was required. I wasn't exactly certain what we were going to do, but I knew we couldn't afford another night like that one.

The next morning, Greg and I decided to try a much simpler tack. We strolled out, bought stacks of soft porn magazines, and began ringing up every single massage service or escort agency advertised at the back of these publications. We processed the girls like a factory conveyor belt, one every ten minutes. No, we weren't feeling lonely. We just knew that many of these agencies were owned by the same businessmen. That meant that some of them would surely have been hired in the past few days by members of the Saudi entourage.

God knows what the porter thought as he watched this procession of girls coming up to our rooms. At one stage, I walked down to the lobby for a change of scene, only to be confronted by the elderly bellhop I'd asked about 'the action' the night before. He gave me an exaggerated wink and a smile, as if to say 'You lucky bastard.' If only he'd known the truth of the matter. Maybe he was reflecting on all the business he could have had if he'd reacted to my earlier probe. On the other hand, perhaps he just thought I was insatiable.

By mid-afternoon, I was getting pretty bored of 'French, hand or full sex . . . blah . . . blah . . . blah . . . ' and total non-reactions when I started questioning the girls on their previous customers. Most of them were either too thick or too scared I was a cop to say anything. One girl nearly caused an awful scene when she waltzed straight into my room, stripped off and jumped in the bath, insisting I joined her. When I told her I'd left my money at work she threatened to get her pimp to beat me up unless I coughed up some cash. Finally, she believed my story and stormed out of the room. I never even bothered to ask her about Arabs. It didn't seem worth it.

I'd just finished with girl number ten (or maybe it was twenty) when there was a knock on my door. I felt I was holding an audition for a London show using a bed instead of a stage. At the end of each session, it was tempting to say 'Next', which would have saved me having to get up to open the door yet again. But I really didn't want to rub these girls up the wrong way, so I just carried on getting up and down, opening and shutting the door to my army of female companions.

Anyway, on to number eleven. I opened the door and realised this broad was in a different class from her predecessors.

To start with, she said hello in an extraordinary German accent. She was also wearing a real fur coat that looked as if it probably cost a few dozen through-the-night sessions with the entire Saudi Arabian touring party. I was slightly taken aback. She just didn't look the part. She didn't have a brassy voice, she wasn't dressed in skin-tight clothes, she just didn't look as if she'd just walked out of the Purple Pussycat Club in Hemel Hempstead.

She must have noticed the slightly quizzical look on my face because she immediately started small-talking – something prostitutes don't tend to bother with. A whole variety of subjects were covered over the next ten minutes, including the weather, how much the hotel cost and what I did for a job. I said publishing, and my name was John, naturally. Then I began asking her questions and she told me she lived in Esher, had one son at boarding school and drove a BMW. This was no ordinary prostitute – remember, this was before yuppies took over and BMWs became two-a-penny.

Why, I asked, was she a working girl if she was already so well off?

'Oh, I am so bored at home. My husband doesn't like me working so I do this instead. It gives me some pocket money and I enjoy it. It's dangerous and fun. I like taking risks.'

Despite all this pleasant banter, my new German friend from Esher was out to earn a crust and get a kick or two. She suddenly looked at her watch and said: 'Now, come on, John. How do you want it?' I had almost forgotten what she was here for, but that comment snapped me into action. This was always the difficult bit. She muttered something about £100 for straight sex so I took the bait and looked at my watch.

'Well, actually, I hadn't realised the time myself. Look, here's the money. I'm sorry, but that's the way it goes, I guess.' I smiled weakly. I knew I had to get rid of this girl otherwise she was going to smell a rat. But I still hadn't asked the right questions, so I joked: 'You ought to work for some of these Saudi Arabians staying here at the moment. They must be worth a fortune.'

'Oh,' she said ever so casually, 'I went with three of them yesterday afternoon. I hate them. I don't ever want to work for Arabs again. They're so dirty and horrible.'

Bingo! I had stumbled upon the girl of my dreams (in a journalistic sense, of course).

The problem I now had was to hold on to this girl while I pumped her – I mean, interviewed her. She was itching to go and, I think, was slightly disappointed that I hadn't done the

138

business. Then I had a brain wave. Out came the trusted wallet, and I blurted out pretending to be embarrassed: 'Just talk to me about what they did to you.'

It worked a treat. She got £100 and I got all the sordid detail. Most of it was too pornographic to publish. It had been so easy to extract – and when I thought of all that chaos the night before . . . Here I was getting exactly what I wanted without having eight whisky-sodden hacks lying slumped in armchairs scattered round the hotel lobby.

That night I managed to locate a casino where a number of the Khaled entourage had been the previous night – and lost thousands, according to the manager. So far I had scored two out of three; I just had to confirm they'd been drinking too, and I'd be home and dry.

By late the next day, I'd managed to get a barman in a local pub to confirm that the Arabs had been in drinking. God knows if they were the same ones I'd been pursuing, but it was pretty obvious that some of my lot must have had a drink, or so I thought. Then I spotted a couple of them supping lagers in the bar of the hotel. Everything was now in place for me to do a cracking story along exactly the lines PJ wanted. That was the signal for me to begin coasting on the story. That means Greg and I took it easy and enjoyed a number of the hotel's finest dishes – food, that is! We had become like regular customers in the hotel, and were almost on first-name terms with some of the staff. It was Thursday afternoon when I phoned over my story from the hotel bedroom, delighted in getting everything complete so early in the week. It was the biggest mistake I made in my entire life.

I rang home, as I did every day when I was away, and my wife Clare answered: 'Something weird is going on here. We've had people taking pictures of the house,' she said.

I didn't know what she was going on about. 'Maybe it was an estate agent?' I said.

'No, they were Arab looking types,' she replied.

Suddenly I started to worry. Maybe someone had sussed me out at the hotel. After all we had been rather conspicuous.

'Do you think it's to do with the story you're on,' asked Clare.

I was convinced it was. I wanted to get home as quick as possible. I told Clare to ring the police and I got on the phone to PJ. He told me to go home immediately and sent a freelance journalist to act as a minder until I arrived back in Wimbledon.

I drove home at breakneck speed. There was no doubt in my mind about what had happened. The Saudis had worked out who I was. I was such a fool. I had been openly phoning the office from the hotel and I'd even filed the story over the phone from my room.

When I finally got to the house, it looked very quiet from the outside. I began to worry that perhaps the Arabs had come back and kidnapped Clare and the kids. It was a ridiculous way to think, but I knew that crossing wealthy, powerful people was a dangerous business.

Once inside, I found everyone safe and my PJ-appointed minder – an old and experienced hand – up to his ears in . . . bathing the kids! It was a wonderful sight to see this professional journalist with his shirtsleeves rolled up playing bubble bath with three tiny kids.

We never did get to the bottom of it. All we knew was that three Arab-looking characters, carrying a camera on a tripod, stopped outside my house and proceeded to take loads of snaps of the property. When asked by a neighbour what they were doing, they said they were tourists and walked off towards a Mercedes parked nearby. I cannot imagine many tourists being interested in turn-of-the-century terraced houses in downtown Wimbledon.

Two days later, my family having survived their brush with the mystery Arab hit-men, the *Sunday Mirror* duly published my masterpiece entitled KHALED'S SEXY SHEIKS. CALL GIRLS CASH IN AS BIG SPENDING ARABS GO OUT ON THE TOWN.

We didn't cause a diplomatic incident on the scale of the Death of a Princess row, but we must have made Khaled and his men splutter over their cornflakes that Sunday morning.

EIGHT
The Italian Stallion

ONE OF THE GREATEST FEELINGS YOU CAN HAVE IS WHEN you get a job that will set you up for life in a career you are determined to follow. It happened to me one Tuesday in 1980, when P.J. Wilson rang me at home to say: 'The job's yours if you want it, mate.' I'd spent two tough years freelancing for the *Sunday Mirror*, and this was my reward – a staff job on one of the biggest selling papers in the land.

Within minutes of the call, I was on my way to the office to start my first day as a permanent staffer. It was my dream come true. I kept thinking about all those front-page bylines I was going to get from now on, those glamorous assignments abroad. As a freelance reporter, I'd often sweated blood on a story only to find the staff men got all the glory and the byline. Now it was my turn and I was truly relishing the opportunity. At just twenty-two years of age I was one of the youngest staff men in Fleet Street, but as I'd left school at sixteen I didn't feel inexperienced. I was a little apprehensive, but when I walked into the office, PJ yelled: 'Welcome on board, Wense,' and immediately my anxiety turned to pride. I didn't have long to bask in the glorious feeling of being a Fleet Street reporter at my own desk for long, though. I'd barely settled in when my line went. It was one of the newsdesk secretaries.

'There's a woman on the line says she wants to expose a prison chef. PJ said you should talk to her.'

Newspapers are constantly bombarded by callers, many of whom turn out to be complete and utter nutters, or at best time-wasters who just make things up because they're feeling lonely and want to talk to someone. I once went to meet a man who rang the paper and insisted he knew who the next double agent after Anthony Blunt was. Unfortunately he sounded so plausible on the phone that we couldn't take the risk of ignoring him. I was dispatched to a disused railway yard in North London to meet our Deep Throat. It was a really corny location, and I was convinced this man had been watching too many spy movies.

I hung around in the yard for about forty minutes, getting soaking wet, waiting for a guy whom my News Editor believed might be our key to fame and fortune. Eventually I heard a rustling in the distance and a tiny, shadowy figure appeared. It was difficult to make out his features, but as he approached me my remaining optimism evaporated. Standing before me was a five-foot midget who looked remarkably like a tramp. Hardly the sort of person you expect to have inside information on MI6.

'Did I speak to you on the phone?' It was difficult to conceal my disbelief.

'Yeah. I know who he is, you know.'

There was no way this bizarre little dwarf had anything worth knowing so I decided I'd scarper at the first opportunity. But I didn't want to upset him because . . . well, remember the dwarf in *Don't Look Now*?

'So you know who he is?' I tried to play along while I scrambled around in my mind for an easy exit.

'But I want twenty thousand quid up front.'

Surprise, surprise. He wants £20,000 (in used notes no doubt) before he'll even tell me the name. I think I've heard this one before.

I felt like saying 'Piss off', but that might have sparked off an ugly incident. After all, I didn't know what vicious weapons he might be hiding in his tatty duffle coat.

'I'll tell you what,' I told him. 'For clearance of that sort of cash I'll have to pop down to the phone and ring my boss to get his OK.'

I didn't bother to wait for a reply, I just strolled out of that yard and prayed that I'd never bump into that particular gentleman ever again. Amazingly, he rang the office six more times before getting the message that we weren't interested in his amazing exposé.

Our midget friend wasn't the only nutter I came across. On another occasion a man rang in to say he had evidence that a particular MP was a paedophile. I was in a filthy mood when I took the call and very scathing about his claims. But the man insisted on meeting me at a pub on Blackfriars Bridge, so I went along, just in case he was the genuine article. I knew he was going to be a pain in the arse from the moment I met him. He let me buy the first drink – and every subsequent one – which is a sure sign that your contact is broke, and that in turn usually means he's a conman. When I asked him outright what evidence he had to back his story, he accused me of not believing him. That was all I needed to turn nasty. In the end I got in such a strop with him that I walked out of the pub. If I'd been in better mood, I would have listened more intently and perhaps arranged another meeting. After all, if there was even a shred of truth in what he was saying, then it was political dynamite. But sometimes you just have to trust your instincts.

Three weeks later the same man completely conned another tabloid into running a very dodgy story which almost cost them a fortune in libel, so my instinct about him turned out to be right. But every now and again a real story comes in via a phone call out of the blue, and you have to learn to tell the diamonds from the paste – even if that means chasing after a lot of nonsense nine times out of ten.

Since this was my first full day in the job I was brimful of enthusiasm as the secretary transferred this prison-scandal woman over to my phone line – at least she would get a fair chance. Too many reporters in Fleet Street treat these sort of calls with contempt (as I would myself in a few years time), and I'm convinced they end up missing out on a lot of fantastic stories as a result.

'Hello, there's a prison chef where I've just been inside and he's recruiting girls as prostitutes once they get out – '

'Hang on a minute, let's start at the beginning, OK?' I said.

My informant poured out all the details about a chef at a

women's prison who went under the nickname of the 'Italian Stallion' – I don't need to tell you why. He had been chatting up the inmates and then offering to pimp for them once they got out, she claimed. This woman even alleged that he screwed them in the prison kitchens, 'just to make them feel indebted to him'. But it was the fact he was said to be 'selling' these girls as prostitutes that really interested me. It was a sensational story if true, but I hadn't even established this woman's identity yet. And since she was an ex-inmate herself, there had to be some doubt about her own honesty, to put it mildly.

'I would like to meet you,' I said.

There was silence on the other end of the line, then she told me: 'I don't want to get involved.'

This is unfortunately, a familiar line from people who call in to newspapers. For some reason they think they can tell you something anonymously and then disappear. What they don't realise is that you need evidence – without it there is no point in pursuing such stories.

'Look, there's nothing I can do with this story if you don't meet me,' I said firmly but patiently. After some more gentle persuasion she agreed to see me and within minutes I was on my way to the highly unlikely location of Pease Pottage – a tiny, scruffy village just literally on the edge of the M23 in Sussex.

Carol was her name, and her picturesque 1960s council house oozed with all the olde worlde charm of a Beefeater Steak House at a motorway service station. The inside of the house had a distinctly doggy odour, but fortunately there was no sign of the dog. She made me a cup of tea which I graciously accepted.

Carol was the salt of the earth, really. She'd been locked up inside for six months for a variety of petty offences and seemed to have lived a rather full life both in and out of jail. She casually told me how she had indulged in lesbian sex with other inmates and been given one by the randy prison chef up against the pantry door. She had even smoked pot for the first time and described it as a 'real laugh'. Carol also admitted rather disarmingly:

'I loved it inside. It's much better than being free again. There's always someone to take the pressure off you inside. Here, I've got the kids and the house to worry about. Daft, innit?'

In a strange sort of way I understood exactly what she meant by those remarks. There was a marvellous logic about virtually everything she said. But I have to admit I was beginning to wonder about this woman and her story. Perhaps the whole thing was an elaborate fantasy she'd dreamed up while a guest of Her Majesty.

As I sat on the imitation leather sofa in her lounge I decided not to beat about the bush and told her that if she wanted to expose this man then the *Sunday Mirror* was the perfect platform. Carol supplied me with all the details she could think of. The prison chef's name and address; other inmates' names and addresses since being released, even her own date of birth – which I asked her because I knew I could check this elsewhere. If she was lying about her personal details, then there was little chance she was telling the truth about the story.

What made me inclined to believe her, though, was that she didn't ask for any money. Now that is unusual! Still, like the typical tabloid operator I was trying to be, I felt I had to delve deeper and find out what her real motivation was. Nobody turns over a former lover and a load of fellow prisoners without having a good reason. The more I thought about it, the more I realised I was going to have to be careful with this one.

Besides checking her date of birth, I could also give what information I had to my special crime contact, who would then get his tame cop to check her through on the police national computer. This was a highly illegal thing to do, but for £25 a name it was very good value from a newspaper's point of view. What it would show was whether she had in fact been jailed, and when.

Most papers in Fleet Street have ways of gaining access to the police computer via a friendly cop who gets a bottle of scotch or a few notes in return. Over the years there has been much controversy over the illegal use of the police computer, and every now and again there is a supposed crackdown by Scotland Yard. There was once a massive court case about a gambling club that allegedly took the car registration numbers of punters at the club, checked them through a friendly policeman and then chased these customers if they got behind with their gambling debts. It caused an outcry, and the Yard claimed they were stamping out such illegal practices. All I can say is that while this was going on my police computer checking service continued untouched. Where there's a will there's a way, and where there's a cash reward there's always a slightly bent cop willing to help a friendly journalist. A criminal records check can be achieved if you give your friendly cop the date of birth, approximate height, and hair colour of your subject. Within twenty-four hours he will come back with a record of every criminal offence ever committed by that person. It can prove very handy. The only time when it is difficult to check a car registration or phone number is if the subject is a well-known politician or civil servant. The Yard has introduced a security coding system for such people, and when they are checked independently by a policeman the computer makes him record his name alongside the request for information. That means the officer can be traced by his superiors, and there is no way a copper is going to risk that.

Anyway, Carol and I talked and talked about her amazing claims. She stuck rigidly to her guns and never faltered – I could find no holes in her story so far. She gave me all the salacious details: what the chef did to her, how he approached her when she was due for release and suggested they meet; how he kept in touch with other inmates; the drugs; the sex; the lot. Carol didn't flinch as she explained some of the extraordinary incidents involving her and other frustrated women inmates.

By the time I left her home some three hours later, I was convinced that Carol was telling the truth – and the subsequent police checks proved positive as well. She had been in prison for the crimes she'd mentioned to me, and all her personal details tallied perfectly.

The Italian Stallion

When I rang PJ from a windswept phone box at a service station, his reaction was, as per normal, ecstatic. 'I told you we'd start you off on the big one, mate. We'll rap this one up in a couple of weeks,' he told me.

The next day I went into the office to gather a team to help me on this marvellous tale of sex and drugs in a women's prison, made even more juicy by the fact that this particular jail held some of the most notorious women criminals in Britain. Our special investigations unit consisted of myself and a senior staff man, plus a female reporter, because PJ, as ever, was convinced that only a woman could interview another woman about sensitive things like sex. (In my experience the opposite is often the case. Many women love to talk about their bedroom activities in front of men. No doubt there is an ulterior motive, but who cares?) There was also a freelance 'runner' in the team to run errands.

We then began the long and arduous task of interviewing as many former inmates as possible to get evidence to back Carol's claims. It was a very slow process. Addresses often proved to be incorrect or out of date – after all, we were dealing with ex-cons. We took five days tracking down one mugger who'd just been released from the jail. When we finally got the the correct address in a highly dodgy area of Dagenham, myself and our freelance knocked on the door, hopeful of scoring a direct hit for once. This time, I'm afraid, my knack of looking like a police officer spoiled our chance. Within thirty seconds of our third rather heavy-handed knock, I spotted a figure climbing over the fence at the side of the gate and running off down an alleyway. Like any self-respecting police officer, I gave chase, determined she wouldn't get away as she looked distinctly like the person we were after.

After a five-hundred-yard chase I got close enough to bellow out my name and newspaper. Luckily, my subject immediately responded in a way that was music to my ears.

'Newspapers. Cor! I could be famous.'

She stopped in her tracks and an inquisitive smile came over her face. It was just the sort of reaction you get from people in certain walks of life, and that was good news from my point of view. Another stroke of luck then came our way. This jailbird punter spotted my female companion and was immediately bowled over by her looks. At that particular moment neither of us even noticed the way this former mugger was eyeing up my colleague. But it became painfully clear when we were all sitting down for a meal at a Little Chef that night and she started stroking this attractive reporter's leg under the table. To be quite honest, even if I had known what was going through this woman's mind, I think I would have just turned a blind eye and failed to alert my co-reporter. I was that desperate to make sure we got her side of the story.

The girl told us all about the Italian Stallion, drug-taking, and every other vice that kept the inmates entertained. This prison was rapidly beginning to sound more like a holiday camp than one of Her Majesty's finest jails. By the end of the meal, Babs (that really was her name) had given us the sort of material needed, and had even promised to sign a sworn statement confirming all the details. It was all a bit of a joke, really, as Babs couldn't read or write. But we knew that just so long as we got her scrawl on the bottom right-hand corner of each piece of paper we would be home and dry.

The other achievement of the evening was the fact that the waitress at the Little Chef gave me a blank receipt – a licence to create my expenses the following week or whenever I got a chance to do them. All in all it had been a most satisfactory day's work.

We got some fascinating stories from Babs about the Italian Stallion. 'He used to do body searches on girls while looking for stolen sugar or coffee,' she told us. And: 'He would regularly walk round the prison kitchens stripped to the waist. We used to chase each other round the kitchen for fun. We would nearly always let him catch us.'

It was great stuff, but we still lacked the crucial evidence to support Carol's claim that Stallion was recruiting girls and pimping for them once they got outside. No matter how hard we tried, we could not get confirmation of this from any of the girls we interviewed. On one weekend I spent forty-eight hours doorstepping the home of one former inmate, who was clearly on the game. But when she finally emerged from her North London tower-block home – after ten men had been in and out of her flat – she still denied even being a prostitute, insisting instead on describing herself as an actress and model. She was a 'working' girl, but she didn't want her friends or family to know. I suppose that is perfectly reasonable, but it wasn't any consolation to us at that moment.

The only person who'd claimed that the prison chef was into prostitution was our original informant, Carol. But PJ was determined that we got more evidence. We'd been on the story for about six weeks already, but he just kept saying: 'We've got to prove the prostitution. Otherwise it's only half a story.'

So we kept going back to Carol and she would point us in the direction of more ex-inmates, but still none of them could give us a sworn statement saying the Stallion had set them up in business.

At one stage, I really thought we had cracked it. I found myself waiting with another reporter outside a tower block in St John's Wood. We were on the trail of a girl who'd been jailed for soliciting and had been inside with Carol. When she finally turned up at four in the morning we had to pretend we were two punters out for a good time in order to get her to let us go up to her flat. Then all she could offer us was fifteen minutes on the eighteenth floor of a tower block for a flat fee of £100. When we told her who we were she attacked my colleague with a knife and we ran out of the front door in something of a hurry. I think she was irritated – to say the least – that we weren't a couple of blokes who wanted a threesome. I suppose you can't blame her: if you were a prostitute and two blokes asked you if they could come upstairs for a chat, what would you think? We were just relieved that we didn't take her up on her generous offer of 'two-up for £100'. But, not surprisingly, we were becoming increasingly sceptical about the entire story. Here was yet another woman who denied all knowledge of Carol, Stallion, and everything else to do with our investigation. If a self-confessed prostitute wouldn't say she was recruited by the Stallion, then there had to be something wrong with the information.

By week ten, the entire prison vice investigation team was growing weary to say the least. PJ was, as ever, still very buoyant, but his enthusiasm was not having the desired effect. Then, on my fifth check-in phone call of another fruitless day, he had a brainwave. It was an idea that only PJ could possibly think would work, but at least it gave us the chance of a result. He knew he had to salvage this story somehow. The Editor would be furious if he admitted a team of highly-paid (his words, not mine) journalists had wasted ten weeks travelling round the country interviewing ex-jailbirds about a story that didn't stand up.

PJ's plan was simple. We just had to get Carol to contact the Italian Stallion and ask him over to her place for a meeting. During that get-together in Pease Pottage, she would have to turn the conversation towards pimping and prostitution. We would have the entire ground floor heavily bugged and that would enable us to get the incriminating evidence we needed. As usual, it sounded very easy, but in reality . . .

Carol liked the plan. She seemed eager for revenge on the Stallion – I never did get to the bottom of her motives for telling us about the vice ring in the first place. I didn't even suspect anything when, on the day in question, she was wearing a slinky, silky dress slashed to the hip. I should have known better.

Anyway, the scene was set. Myself and the team had managed to hire more than £1,000 worth of highly sophisticated bugging equipment, most of which we didn't have a clue how to operate. PJ said no expense should be spared. He knew this had to work for all our sakes. I felt very much the same way since if he went I probably would as well.

In a white hired Transit van, we had proceeded to good old Pease Pottage to set up our equipment at Carol's house, just hours before the Stallion's scheduled arrival.

The original plan was to sit in the reasonably spacious van

about three hundred yards from the house and listen through all our strategically positioned bugging devices. But it turned out the van was useless for reception, so we re-set up in the tiny boxroom that Carol optimistically described as a spare bedroom. From this vantage point we could monitor everything electronically and my photographer could get a perfect view of the front garden, where he hoped to snap Stallion and Carol together. Before positioning ourselves in the room, we made sure all eight of the bugging devices were working. There were three in subtle places – hidden in a bunch of roses, behind a picture, and stuck to the phone in the room Carol described as her lounge. She had assured us she would take him in there for their little chat. Then we made her put one in her bra. It seemed a safe enough place at the time. I still hadn't given any thought to that slinky dress. Another four bugs were scattered round the hallway and kitchen just in case they talked in other areas besides the lounge.

Carol seemed very excited about the prospect of seeing Stallion again. She was oozing with charm, or so I thought. I have to say I was bit surprised when she poured herself a quadruple Bacardi and coke before he'd even arrived. But I put this down to nerves. I couldn't have been further from the truth.

Anyway, myself and the photographer assembled at the appointed time in our little cubicle and waited for the arrival of Stallion. The sun was beating down on our side of the house and it was blisteringly hot, but I had my orders and wasn't about to go AWOL on this one.

We heard a car pulling up and Carol looked out of the window.

'It's him,' she screeched.

We shut the door to the room, switched on our mass of monitoring gear which crackled with static, and waited. I was terrified that none of this gadgetry would actually work, but then I heard the rustle of Carol's dress and her heavy breathing.

Harry, the snapper, poked his lens directly out between the curtains and whispered a running commentary for me: 'He's got out the car. Now he's walking towards her . . . ' He needn't have bothered, as I was wearing headphones linked to that vital bug in Carol's bra.

'Great, I've got some fantastic snaps,' yelled Harry.

'Shhhh. They'll hear you,' I prodded him and put my finger to my lips.

'Would you like a nip of Vodka? I know it's your favourite,' and replies like, 'That would be lovely Carol' were the only bits of conversation to start with. Carol had already drunk about a quarter of a bottle of Bacardi, and I hoped she wasn't going to forget her lines. There hadn't yet been any reference to prostitution, but then I presumed she would have to coax it out of him gently, so I wasn't worried – yet.

Soon the little pre-planned gathering had moved to the lounge. When the pair of them sat down there was a rustling like a flock of sparrows in a hollybush, but I thought nothing of it as these sort of bugs picked up every noise. I could even hear the rubbing noise of their bottoms settling on Carol's PVC-covered sofa. Carol, who in the long tradition of working women had omitted to wear tights or stockings under her dress, made a particularly odd noise when her bare thighs rubbed against the plastic. By this time Harry the snapper had picked up the spare set of headphones to listen alongside me. Carol then got up to go to the kitchen to refill Stallion's glass with Vodka and orange. All alcohol had been supplied by us. On reflection that may have been a mistake.

Talk had been highly innocuous up to this point, and we were beginning to get impatient. Then they stopped chatting and I thought I heard a squelching sound. Still no conversation.

'What the fuck are they up to?' I whispered to Harry.

More squelching noises, and now a sucking sound.

'I think they're snogging, old boy,' Harry replied.

And I thought she was supposed to be prising an admission of dirty deeds out of him, not performing them!

Then the rustling and squelching stopped and Carol said delicately: 'I must just go to the toilet.'

Thank God, I thought, she's seen sense and broken the

whole kissing session up by going to the loo. Once she got inside the lavatory, I realised I was very much mistaken. There was an ear-shattering whoosh and crash and I ripped off my earphones because the noise was so bad. My snapper did likewise. Then everything went dead. Carol had flushed the bra-bug down the loo. Meanwhile, the lounge bugs had picked up the distinct sound of flies being zipped undone. This wasn't looking good for us.

The three lounge bugs picked up her voice again: 'Come here, you randy bastard.'

It was Carol, thoughtfully giving us a commentary. We didn't need any more sound effects to know what would happen next.

Harry and I sat there dumbfounded as we heard the squeaky sound of bare skin on plastic. They had obviously both stripped off. And now they were bonking at a furious pace. This went on for at least thirty minutes and I have to say it sounded as if Carol knew what she was doing.

Eventually there was a chorus of ooohs and aahs as they reached a climax. I felt only relief that it was all over. Perhaps Carol might now get on with the business at hand?

The temperature in our little room must have been in the nineties and, to make matters worse, we were afraid to move a muscle for fear that Stallion might hear us.

'Perhaps she'll get on with it now,' I whispered hopefully to Harry. But it was not to be.

'I want more – now!'

Carol was in ecstasy, and nothing was going to stop her enjoying every moment. She either got a kick out of knowing that we were listening to every movement, or she just felt the urge to be thoroughly serviced and didn't give a damn who knew.

To cut a long story short, Carol and Stallion went on like this for several hours. Each time one of them climaxed the other would say 'More!' And each time this happened, Harry and I would turn to each other with a look of disbelief on our faces and utter the immortal words: 'Oh fuck.'

It was now like the Gobi desert in that room, and the pair of us were no doubt far weaker than the two bonking rabbits downstairs, despite the fact we were doing nothing more than listening to two people copulating. The worst part was that we had to concentrate on every word, however obscene, just in case he made reference to prostitution. It was all thoroughly exhausting.

By early evening we were fading fast. Then mercifully Stallion announced: 'I must get off home, Carol.' You could feel the relief in our tiny room. Just a few zip-fastening minutes later and Carol was waving a fond farewell to the man she had earlier described as evil. I really did wonder if she set the whole thing up because she wanted to be fucked rigid by the Italian Stallion.

Once downstairs, Carol looked me straight in the eye and said: 'I tried everything to get him to talk about it. But he's just a bit too clever. Do you think he knew the room was bugged?'

Well, she certainly tried everything, but not exactly in the way I'd intended.

Amazingly, Carol didn't seem in the slightest bit embarrassed by the fact that we'd listened to her every move for all that time. Then I realised the reason why. She was as pissed as a fart and if we hadn't got out of that house double fast then I don't doubt that one of us would have ended up replacing the Stallion in her affections.

I was distraught. We'd failed to find any evidence for the prostitution story and the whole project was a disaster. All we had was a tape of a former prison inmate being given the most severe bonking of her life by a man who worked as a prison chef. But when I rang the newsdesk, they were far from despondent.

'Well done, mate,' said one of my esteemed leaders. 'It would have been great to stand up the prostitution line, but we've still got the randy chef breaking prison rules by screwing an ex-inmate. And all the drug-taking and lesbian sex from the other inmates. It'll make a great piece.'

I was still somewhat befuddled by the sexual antics of Carol and Stallion. I was haunted by the screeching noise of bare flesh on a plastic settee. It is a sound I think I am unlikely ever to hear again.

Just a few days later the *Sunday Mirror* splashed the SCANDAL OF THE PRISON ROMEO, with a photo of Carol and Stallion with another headline over it saying CAUGHT BEFORE THE ACT. It was perfect tabloid fodder. If only we'd been able to print the full story of what we went through to get the story.

NINE
Are You Sure You Didn't Kill Him?

JOURNALISTS ARE MOODY BASTARDS AT THE BEST OF times. It is the very nature of the job, I suppose. Up one minute when a story is going well, down the next when the whole article crumbles in a heap around you. There is no way of predicting what is going to happen when you set out on a particular story, and that leaves you vulnerable to depression when things don't turn out the way you want them to. We may seem a ruthless bunch to the outside world, but we are still human after all. Even hard-bitten hacks have a heart, and sometimes even a conscience. Inevitably things happen to you occasionally that really make you think twice about ignoring people's feelings – events that ruin other people's lives and leave you with a sick feeling in the stomach.

It was the feeling I got when I covered a very disturbing story in the autumn of 1982.

Property developer's wife Linda Sturley had gone missing and the whole world was convinced, mainly as a result of vicious innuendo, that husband Graham had done the dirty deed. It was, by all accounts, the perfect tabloid story. No trace of the wife had been found and hubby had moved a new girlfriend into the family home just a few days after his wife's 'disappearance'. The neighbours had decided he'd done it, and the whole of Britain was gradually following suit – thanks to the popular press. Nobody actually said he'd buried her body in the garden, but it wasn't difficult to read between the lines.

This outrageous whodunnit became the biggest running story of late summer that year. Every tabloid in the land was camped on the Sturley doorstep in Biggin Hill, Kent. It had all the perfect ingredients: respectable, homely wife (she worked

156

as an Avon lady in her spare time), two young children, husband seemingly fairly wealthy and successful (by tabloid standards that meant a detached home in the suburbs). Yet she'd just upped and left home, or so he claimed.

The husband was making life difficult for himself, though. He just wasn't distraught enough. In fact he seemed rather relieved. As well as the newly ensconced mistress in his home, there were her two young children, also now part of the Sturley family circle.

The beauty of this story from a tabloid point of view was that there was no body, so therefore no one could be charged. That meant we could write what the hell we liked about the case. All sorts of angles were covered by the papers, including, naturally, a denial from hubby that he had anything to do with his wife's disappearance.

Then the police obligingly announced they were going to dig up the entire garden of the Sturley bungalow. It was blatantly obvious they thought he'd buried her there. The tabloids (and television) had a field day as virtually every shovel-load was analysed by police and press alike.

Unlike most running stories, which eventually dwindle into nothing, this one just kept gaining strength. Nearly every day some new article about the Sturleys would appear. It was relentless. Mrs Sturley's mum would open up her heart about the rumours; another relative would start pointing the finger; a photo of the mistress would be released to the papers; and so it went on.

It was therefore no surprise when my News Editor on the *Mail on Sunday*, where I worked at the time, sent me down to Biggin Hill one wet and windy Friday afternoon. However, what he gave me before my departure was unusual: it was a copy of a police statement made by Sturley in which he confessed to hitting his wife on a number of occasions on the night before her disappearance.

The implications of this statement were enormous. What he had admitted to was perilously close to a full confession. Yet obviously he had refused to buckle under police interrogation, so all they had was this admission that he had hit her. It was made very clear to me that our crime correspondent had been 'lent' the statement by the police, furious that they had failed to find enough evidence to arrest Sturley. This sort of thing happened quite frequently in Fleet Street. The police would become frustrated at not being able to arrest a certain person, so they would leak the facts behind the case to one of their friendly correspondents on the national papers, in the hope that tabloid pressure would get results. A lot of these leaks never actually materialise into stories because the subject matter is so sensational that no paper dares print it, even though it has come from the horse's mouth, so to speak.

Two of the most classic cases that spring to mind involved high-ranking politicians. Every tabloid in Fleet Street has, at one time or another, tried to prove that a certain MP is fond of importuning men in lavatories near to the Houses of Parliament. This man has been cautioned no less than five times by police, but he has never been charged because he has always managed to call on friends in high places to step in and make sure his name is wiped from the Scotland Yard computer. The local police got so furious that they approached a well known crime reporter on one of the tabloids and offered him the story on a plate. They even handed over copies of statements made by the MP in which he admitted he had a 'problem'. The paper in question then mounted a massive operation to prove that this MP was up to no good.

They started with a round-the-clock watch on his London home. After weeks of surveillance, there wasn't a shred of evidence, so the journalists started making door-to-door inquiries amongst his political enemies. Unfortunately that turned out to be a very silly move because, however much they might shout across the House of Commons at each other, most MPs are actually on good terms with each other and tend to stick together at times like these.

The next move was to doorstep the country home of the said MP. That proved just as fruitless, as the MP's constituents also closed ranks. The newshounds were hampered by the fact that they could hardly go around asking people if such and such an MP enjoyed the company of rent boys. They had to do it in a far more roundabout sort of way, with odd questions like: 'Do you every recall Mr So and So being in the company of a girlfriend?' The hoped-for answer would go something along these lines: 'Oh no. I've never seen him with a girl, but he does seem to get out with a lot of young men.' Of course, the answer never actually came like that. Instead it was usually a terse reply like: 'Why don't you ask him yourself?'

Anyway, the journos then turned to their last resort and actually doorstepped this dodgy MP for weeks, trying to prompt a response from him personally. But they failed to get near him. At one stage, two reporters called at his London home to be told by his maid that he was at his country home, while, in fact, they could clearly see the MP in his front room. But there was nothing they could do. He knew what they were up to, but he also knew they would never print the story without an admission from him. He was right, of course, and that story is still going the rounds in what's left of Fleet Street. Every now and again a paper makes an attempt to stand the story up, then fails – and gives up trying. Meanwhile the MP is still in an important position of power, and I am personally baffled as to why he hasn't been quietly removed from office. But that's politics, I guess.

The other case involves a photograph in the possession of the obscene publications squad at Scotland Yard. It shows a famous MP, dressed in a Boy Scout uniform with two boys in their early teens in similar attire. The picture has been seen by a number of crime correspondents and they say it is dynamite, but the Yard will only show it around. They won't hand it over because they know that their top brass would be embarrassed. It is not clear whether that is because there are other people in the photo, or because they just don't want to be seen to be encouraging publication of the story. But when news of the photo first emerged, it had Fleet Street hacks flying around in all directions. Teams of scribes were sent to doorstep the man's family but when they got there they found there was one small problem: how could they throw accusations at the MP or his family if they didn't even have a photo to show them?

I got involved in the story some time later when I was investigating the activities of a paedophile magazine, which was being produced from the shabby back room of a house in Dorset. During my enquiries I came across a particularly nasty piece of work, who claimed he was the editor of this unseemly publication. Knowing I was going to expose his activities he decided to 'cough up' and tell all about the sort of people who were registered on his magazine subscription list. The names made fascinating reading. They included a number of showbiz personalities, a couple of members of the aristocracy and, surprise, surprise, a number of politicians including our friend the Boy Scout. Well I got on to the newsdesk within seconds of seeing the list and tried, somewhat naively on reflection, to persuade my News Editor to run a story naming the 'guilty men'. Then he rightly pointed out that the only evidence we had was a type-written list of names that this master pervert could have taken straight out of *Who's Who*.

He was absolutely right, but I still feel it was an incredible coincidence that the Boy Scout's name was on that list. If only the Yard had made that photo public, then a lot of children might never have been subjected to whatever awful things he has been up to since then. I personally believe that the police wanted to make sure that chummy knew they were on to his paedophile habits, and hoped he would stop committing offences for fear of being exposed in the press. I doubt whether it worked, and the MP in question is still probably dressing up in Boy Scout uniform, but it certainly provided some journalists with a great story to dine out on.

On this story too I had a very delicate problem on my hands. My News Editor desperately wanted me to get Graham Sturley to confess to hitting his wife, but he didn't want me to let on that we had seen the police statement, as it was highly illegal for us to have even read it, let alone have a copy. All I could do was memorise the statement and put all the salient points to Sturley in the hope he would tell all. The idea was that he would believe someone had given us evidence but wouldn't actually know it was the police. We wanted to make sure he didn't complain to the police as that would embarrass all concerned. It was a fairly steep order, I can tell you. I knew the last thing Sturley would want to do was incriminate himself any further – I mean, he might actually have been innocent. Mind you, at that stage the whole world had decided he was guilty as hell.

With the police statement in one pocket and notepad in the other, I set off for deepest Kent. There is something about the Kent side of London that I hate. It always takes hours to get through the south-east London suburbs and the whole area seems like a different world from the rest of the capital. It was where all the black witches came from and where the nastiest murders always took place. Kent never really stood a chance in my eyes. After almost two hours of struggling through the Friday night rush-hour traffic I finally arrived at the Sturley household.

Luckily the story no longer warranted round-the-clock door-stepping as it had been going on for at least two months and no journalist in his right mind hangs around on a story that long. Only one carload of hacks seemed to be parked nearby, and on closer inspection I saw it was occupied by a couple of harmless local news agency blokes hoping to pick up a quick quote from Sturley or his mistress if they left the house. The first thing I did was pump them about what had been happening at the house that day. The reply was, very little indeed. But it was always worth checking. In the past I have got front-page splashes out of innocent agency hacks, unaware that the information they had given me was enough for a 'close friends' type piece. If you cannot get a quote from the subject of a story, then you go for their close friends or relatives. They rarely want to say anything, but sometimes they will talk if you promise not to name them. Hence the description 'close friends'. However, in recent years this process has been extended to gathering as much informa-tion about a person as possible and then quoting an un-named 'close friend' as the source. It adds a touch of credibility, though in reality it means nothing more than that a reporter was too lazy or stupid or clever to bother interviewing the person in question. He or she just hopes and prays that the facts collected along the way are true. The biggest con of all is that popular papers can cover up this subversive behaviour by claiming that they cannot reveal their sources when there is a complaint about a 'close friends' story.

Anyway, there was no need (yet) to use such underhand devices. But I did need to devise a plan to get rid of these loitering agency scribes. I didn't want them hanging around the doorstep when I dropped the punch-up bombshell on Mr Sturley's lap, that was for sure.

'You know he's got a brother,' I lied to one of the young recruits. They looked bemused. I went on: 'He's got a brother who lives in Peckham.' They were beginning to look interested now. 'I've tried his house, but he's never in.' They were starting to bite at the bait, but they definitely needed a bit more encouragement.

'How about the *Mail on Sunday* commissioning you to go over to the brother's house for us now?' I asked in a way they might construe as a command from a top Fleet Street man (me, by the way).

'Why don't you do it yourself?' answered one clever Trevor. I decided to remember his name and face for future reference.

'Well I would, but I've got this very young photographer with me and we need to get a snap of the whole family and, frankly, I don't think he'll manage unless I'm here with him.'

'How much will the *Mail* pay us?' asked clever Trevor.

'A hundred quid,' I made the figure up, and an address in Peckham for these young rookies to fly over to. It worked, and within minutes they had vacated their nest and myself and young snapper were the only ones there. I knew it would take them hours to doorstep the non-address and then return.

We left it another ten minutes in case the agency guys came back and then walked towards the front door of the white bungalow.

It is always a slightly unnerving feeling to be about to knock on someone's door to ask them about a death. It always made me quiver while I was waiting for the door to open.

The first time I ever had to doorstep the victim of a sudden death was on my first week of training on the *Wimbledon News* in South London. I was terrified when the Editor told me to go off and interview the grief-stricken mother of a ten-year-old girl who had died in a road accident just outside her home. When I got to the modest semi, I was too scared to even get out of my car, so I went to the nearest telephone box and rang the office and told my Editor the mother wasn't in. It seemed a much easier option than actually trying to interview her.

'Oh well. Hang on and see if she comes back,' was the reply I had been dreading.

Eventually the mother came out of the house, but I was still too scared to get out of my car and speak to her. Later that day I returned to the office and was told to try ringing her every half-hour until I got through.

'You mustn't give up,' said my Editor. This rookie reporter was terrified. My Editor then stood over me while I rang the number. I'm sure he knew I wasn't actually trying to get hold of the mother. No doubt he'd seen the same thing happen with countless other trainees.

So I went through the ridiculous charade of pretending to dial the number and telling my Editor there was no reply.

'She's probably gone to stay with relatives to try and get over the shock,' I suggested hopefully.

But he wouldn't give up and I spent the next twenty-four hours pretending to ring the mother over and over again as the Editor stood over me, fully aware of the fact that I was shit scared she might answer. Rather unsurprisingly, I never got through. I bet most tabloid journalists have a similar story to tell. We may sometimes seem over-eager for a story, but most of us don't actually revel in the unhappiness of others.

Back at the Sturley household, lights came on in the bunga-low. It was teeming with rain, and footsteps scrunching on the gravel path had obviously alerted the household. It was hardly surprising when Sturley opened the door before we'd even had a chance to knock.

'Yes?' he asked, knowing full well we were journalists from the moment he clapped eyes on us. He must have 'received' hundreds of journalists by that stage, yet he was still smiling. The national press corps had nicknamed him 'the smiling killer'. They said he was a cool customer and they were obviously right.

'I am so sorry to trouble you . . . .' I was using my apologetic interview technique. It normally worked because my humble approach made the punter fell less threatened, even sometimes sorry for poor old me, standing on the step in the pouring rain.

'Come in,' he said charmingly. I couldn't believe it. Here was the man the whole of Britain had been gossiping about, and he'd asked me in without so much as checking my press credentials.

Once inside, snapper and myself were shown to a typically furnished bungalow lounge – frilly curtains, brick-built fireplace, plush pile, twirly patterned carpet, and crying-child style masterpieces hanging from walls that were covered in the sort of paper you normally find in Indian restaurants.

The next half-hour followed the traditional pre-bombshell pattern – talking about everything other than his admission that he'd smashed his wife up just hours before she disappeared. 'Dreadful weather isn't it?' and 'You must be feeling worn out by all this attention?' were just some of the fascinating questions I threw at him to soften him up.

There was no sign of the mistress. Sturley informed us she was bathing the children. It was all very convivial and Sturley was being Mr Charm itself. As he poured us both a cup of steaming hot tea, I found myself wondering if this man really could have cold-bloodedly killed his wife a few months earlier. He seemed such a gentle soul and he was being pleasant to us – two intruders who were aiming to ruin his life in just a few minutes time. He must have known we were up to something, as most of the papers had given up on the story. Yet he never flinched. He didn't even ask us if there was something in particular we needed to talk to him about.

Then I found myself pulling the conversation around to the subject at hand with all the finesse of a demolition derby.

'I understand that you and your wife had a bit of a row the night before she left,' I probed.

'Yes, that's true.'

I couldn't believe the reply. He was admitting it. Normally, when you throw outrageous statements like that at punters they explode and try and kick you out of the house. But the next thirty-odd minutes were breathtaking from a journalistic point of view. He told me how he'd hit and punched his wife in the face and stomach, how he'd accused her of being pregnant by someone else, how he'd moved his mistress and her children into the bungalow just forty-eight hours after his wife went missing.

There was an almost childlike innocence about Sturley that made you believe he really was essentially a very gentle person. I felt no animosity towards him, even though he was openly admitting being a wife-batterer and may even have been guilty of murder.

As if to set the seal on his complete co-operation on the story, he then agreed to pose for photographs with his mistress. Sitting there happily hugging her for the camera, I realised that nothing was going to bring back his wife and, perhaps, there was no real point in ruining the life of this other woman and those innocent children. They really did look genuinely content with life. Maybe everyone was better off than before.

But Sturley's confession represented a major breakthrough in the story, so that by the time we finally pulled out of Biggin Hill that night I was overjoyed. I knew I'd get the front-page splash with this one and even the headline worked brilliantly: I HIT HER . . . BUT I DIDN'T KILL HER it read. It was by far and away the top story in any of the tabloids that Sunday, and I felt justifiably proud of my scoop. Even the Editor was delighted and the daily papers all followed up my story for Monday's editions. This is what newspapers are all about, I thought to myself. A great old-fashioned story was how my colleagues described it. They were still congratulating me when I walked into the office the following Monday for a fresh week of work.

I was really buzzing. It's a great feeling to walk into a newspaper office after you have just written an exceptional splash. But what happened next brought me crashing right back down to earth with an almighty bump.

As I strolled through our sister paper the *Daily Mail*'s office on my way to the paper's reference library, the familiar voice of a newsdesk executive bellowed across the room at me: 'She's named you in the inquest as having killed him.'

I didn't know what he was on about so I went over to the newsdesk. On it was a snap – an urgent piece of text – from the Press Association, a national news agency

The executive looked at me and said: 'Only joking, old son. You did know Sturley was dead, didn't you?'

No, I didn't. I then read how he'd died of a heart attack that day and his mistress was blaming excessive news coverage of the affair as being partly responsible.

I felt dreadful. I actually believed I personally had deprived those kids of a father. The joke about the inquest had been a wind-up, but it had really hit home. I looked and felt numb, and walked back to my office in a daze.

Once at my desk, I turned to a colleague and said: 'Fucking hell, Sturley has died. I feel awful. I feel it's my fault.'

I kept thinking that perhaps I had pushed him too far when I was interviewing him. Perhaps my intense questioning had made Sturley re-live that last night with his wife and brought all those painful memories flooding back. Maybe that caused the stress that killed him.

For the next week I was completely stunned. I couldn't concentrate on my work and I couldn't sleep at night. The spectre of Graham Sturley was haunting me. I have always suffered from a healthy dose of paranoia, but things were now getting out of hand. I fully expected some kind of comeback from his mistress. I might even be asked to appear in the witness box at the inquest . . .

I walked around in the depths of depression, riddled with guilt about the whole episode. At home I was moody and snappy. Every time the phone rang I thought it was going to be Sturley's mistress, their solicitor or, worse still, the coroner. But those calls never came. I hate to imagine how I would have responded if they had.

Yet what was happening to me was nothing compared to the experience of a close friend of mine on another Sunday. She had written a story about a headmaster who had advertised for wife-swapping in a sex magazine and was caught red-handed when the reporter in question posed as a wife-swapper with a male journalist. His name was splashed all over that tabloid and the day the paper came out he walked into woodland near his home and killed himself. It really shook up the normally hard-nosed hackette. She was not only named in the inquest into the headmaster's death, but also received countless threatening phone calls from people who accused her of murdering him. I'll never forget meeting her in a Fleet Street bar after the incident. The guilt had broken her. My problems were trivial in comparison, but I just couldn't shake off the feeling that I'd killed Graham Sturley.

People kept saying things to me like: 'You were only doing your job' or 'It happens all the time.' But that didn't make me feel any better. I still felt guilty.

Perhaps not surprisingly, every paper laid off the story after Sturley's death. I guess we all believed that he had taken the secret of his wife's death to his own grave. But there was no question of harassing the mistress. She had been through enough.

It is impossible to divide up the pressure and stress that contributed to Graham Sturley's death, but it has to be said that the police are partly responsible. After all, they did deliberately release that statement he made in an effort to smoke him out into admitting he murdered his wife. Some officers involved in the case must have been convinced he did kill her, but they couldn't conclusively prove it. They felt that if Sturley admitted hitting his wife publicly then it would only be a matter of time before he confessed to murdering her. But I think someone should have questioned their tactics when he died. They were able to hide behind the cloak of secrecy that they were guaranteed in exchange for handing over the statement to our crime reporter. The police were playing a dangerous game, but no doubt there will be many more deliberate attempts to use the press to put suspects under pressure.

Anyway, none of this will help bring back Graham Sturley.

TEN
The Madonna of the Mountains

I WAS QUIETLY MINDING MY OWN BUSINESS AT MY DESK AT the *Sunday Mirror* one morning when my ears pricked up as I heard good old P.J. Wilson giving somebody a right bollocking on the telephone.

I soon ascertained that it was one of my least favourite colleagues, and no doubt he deserved every word of abuse that was being hurled at him. I disliked this particular hack because he was a lazy and uncommunicative – the sort of guy who never should have been a reporter in the first place. Sure, most of us are lazy at times, but the one thing going for most good reporters is their ability to entertain others with their conversation. This guy couldn't entertain a party of drunks to a piss-up in a brewery.

Anyway, I listened fervently as PJ ripped this fellow to bits – enjoying every second of it but saddened by the fact that the reporter was so thick-skinned he probably didn't even care what PJ was telling him. This bloke had one famous trick he used to pull on virtually every out-of-town assignment he was sent on. He would rush off on the story, then fail to check in with the newsdesk for at least twelve hours, and often more like twenty-four. Eventually, some of us discovered that this journalist was merrily popping down to his girlfriend's home for a quick bonk before heading on to his assignment – well, sometimes. More often than not he would simply stay at his girlfriend's home and pretend he was on a doorstep by ringing in and telling PJ there was 'no sign of life here, mate'. We all slagged him off something rotten because he had a wife and kids tucked away somewhere as well. It's great to be a moralist when you work on a tabloid paper!

Anyway, by the time PJ had slammed the phone down on said hack, it was clear that he had been up to his usual tricks. But by this stage in his career, PJ had begun to suspect the reporter of exactly what the rest of us knew to be true. PJ wouldn't believe what the hack told him, and was having a go at him instead. It was a similar set of circumstances that brought me to the doorstep of megastar Paul McCartney.

What really turned PJ purple with outrage was that the first reporter he sent said to him in a dangerously matter-of-fact way: 'Oh he'll never talk to us anyway.' That was breaking a cardinal rule as far as PJ was concerned. As the eternal optimist, PJ believed there was no one in the world who couldn't be interviewed.

'He's bloody useless. I know he won't even try, mate. I want you to go down and have a crack at it.' PJ had, surprise, surprise, summoned me over to go down on what he described as a 'rescue mission'. Rumours were abounding that Mr and Mrs McC were on the verge of splitting up and, quite reasonably for a tabloid News Editor, PJ wanted to ask the great man himself whether the gossip was true or false. I relished the opportunity. There was no way I could do worse than the other guy, and if I succeeded I would be hailed as a hero. It was the perfect assignment from my point of view.

Within two hours I was outside the secluded country farm-house of the most famous Beatle of them all but – surprise, surprise – there was no sign of my colleague. It was obvious he had never left his mistress's home in the first place. I delighted in telling PJ that his first envoy was not around, but I wasn't quite nasty enough to say where I believed him to be.

For the following four hours I stuck like glue to the entrance gate of the surprisingly modest house waiting for our superstar hero to appear. I had tried shouting over the locked gate. I had even slushed up the muddy drive to within a few yards of the house, but it was all to no avail. The lights were on in the property, but no one was stirring. Looking back on it, it was a pretty daft way to approach Paul McCartney since it wasn't long after the assassination of John Lennon, and it would have been perfectly reasonable to expect the pop star to be somewhat paranoid about uninvited visitors.

But I hung around outside the gates all the same, waiting for an opportunity to grab 'Macca' and squeeze a quote or two out of him. After about four hours had elapsed a car came speeding down the pitch dark country lane towards the house. On a hunch and little else, I got out of my car and stood by the gate as the car slowed down.

It was a bright red Mercedes estate and Paul McCartney was at the wheel. Next to him was wife Linda. That was bad news if I was going to stand the love-rift story up. For a brief moment he looked at me, dishevelled and dripping wet in a Burberry raincoat, and I thought he was going to run me over. Instead the car stopped just a few inches from where I had deliberately stood to prevent him getting into his own house without talking to me.

The electric window slid down and with that inimitable smile, known to millions, he asked me: 'Yes, what can I do for you?' It was a very relaxed approach when you consider it was almost midnight in a lonely country lane – and for all he knew, I might have been a nutter with a gun. I was so shocked he was actually talking to me that I hesitated for a moment, then told him who I was. He seemed relieved and I grabbed at that opportunity.

'I can see from both of you that these marriage-rift stories aren't true.'

'Yep. Load of nonsense,' came the reply from my genial Liverpudlian host.

'I suppose you wish these gossips would stop,' I carried on.

'Yep. Sure do,' came the next reply.

'Would you call them muck-spreaders?' I added.

'Yep.'

'These rumours first surfaced a year ago. They're obviously no more truthful now than then.' I was pushing my luck at this stage.

'Yep. Now why don't you go off home?'

It was my turn to say 'Yep' because that signalled the end of the interview.

Two days later, readers of the *Sunday Mirror* were treated to a marvellous page-three 'Exclusive' headlined: PAUL'S FURY AT LOVE RIFT LIES. The opening paragraphs read:

Superstar Paul McCartney has hit back at the rumours that his marriage is on the rocks.

'I want the world to know that Linda and I are as happy as ever,' he insisted.

'I just wish these gossips would go away and stop talking rubbish.'

Paul, 40, was speaking on the eve of a West German court case in which a 20-year-old girl who says she is his illegitimate daughter is claiming millions of pounds maintenance from him. He was tight lipped about the court case – but with Linda at his side he angrily denied show business rumours of a rift in their 14-year marriage.

'We're targets once again for these malicious muck-spreaders,' he said.

'Last time these rumours started about a year ago and, as you can see, they're no more truthful now than they were then.

Paul spoke exclusively to the Sunday Mirror *at his cottage in the East Sussex countryside, near Rye.*

It was all marvellous tabloid material and I was totally responsible for filing it to the *Sunday Mirror*. But the truth of the matter is that McCartney didn't say much more than a handful of Yeps to me. I then turned the questions into answers on the basis that the essence of what I quoted him as saying was the truth. It is, on reflection, a dangerous method of reporting.

McCartney never complained because this story came into the classic Fleet Street 'evil gossips' syndrome. In other words, put a completely untrue story to a punter and, when they deny it, hey presto, you have the following scenario:

'Pop singer Joe Bloggs last night hit back at the "evil gossips" who are claiming his marriage is over.'

It is a perfect way of squeezing an article out of nothing. You never come back empty-handed!

It was with that very working method firmly in mind that I was dispatched by PJ on one of the silliest stories I ever covered. He had spotted a ludicrous story in the over-the-top American gossip magazine *National Enquirer* about a girl who hadn't eaten anything for *six years*.

Clutching the torn-out cutting in his hand, he briefed me on my mission as if it was the biggest thing since the Profumo Scandal.

'Great story, mate. Bloody fantastic,' were some of the words he used to describe it. I was slightly less sure – except that the girl in question lived in northern Portugal, and I quite fancied a foreign trip at the time. The article claimed that Maria Rosalina Viera had not touched water or food since speaking to Christ six years earlier. She was being hailed by locals in the mountain region east of Oporto as a saint.

Now you might wonder why the *Sunday Mirror* didn't just lift the *Enquirer* story and print it in the paper. But Fleet Street just doesn't work that way. For starters, one tabloid never trusts another tabloid. And, secondly, a staff man will always ensure a good show in the paper, and perhaps provide some new angles. From my point of view, since the story was already written, this trip to Portugal didn't seem too arduous an assignment. Or so I thought . . .

I should have spotted trouble on the horizon when we hit some hairy turbulence on the flight to Oporto. By the time we landed, I was just glad to get my feet on the ground once more. A local photographer had been laid on to greet me and take me to the Madonna of the Mountains. The only problem was that he didn't speak a word of English and his driving was abysmal.

As we twisted and turned round the treacherous mountain roads, I really wondered what the fuck I was doing crammed in a tiny Renault, with a nutty snapper on my way to see a girl who hadn't eaten or drunk anything for six years. I didn't even believe the story in the first place. Half-way through our forty-mile trip, I grabbed the wheel of the car for the umpteenth time, cursed at my photographer friend, and forced him to stop at a café. I needed a drink. My nerves were in shreds – thanks to a bad flight and a bloke whose driving was so bad I wouldn't have trusted him with a tricycle. At the roadside hostelry I downed a whole bottle of wine to ease my fears. Rather surprisingly, my companion didn't touch a drop. But then I'm sure neither of us would have lived to tell the tale if he had.

Slightly pissed and feeling a hundred times better, I climbed aboard for the final stage of our journey to a tiny Portuguese hamlet called Tropeco. As the car scraped the edge of roads that crumbled down mountainsides, I didn't have a care in the world. Alcohol really does sometimes do the trick. Eventually, we reached Tropeco. Or rather, a collection of sheds that wouldn't have looked out of place on a Battersea allotment. The villagers all knew who Maria was. She was a sort of heroine to them, all at the tender age of seventeen.

As the snapper and I scrambled up a muddy bit of hillside towards the shed that we had been told was Maria's home, I got an uncontrollable attack of the giggles. The whole story was ridiculous. It was too silly for words – literally.

I knocked gingerly at the door, expecting a frail figure to beckon us in. After all, you can't have that much energy when you haven't eaten or drunk anything for six years.

Ten minutes later we were still knocking, convinced that Maria might also be hard of hearing because of her Christ-incited starvation. After a further five minutes, I summoned up the courage to try the door of the Madonna of the Mountain's home. It was unlocked, and no one, not even a tiny skinny seventeen-year-old girl, was inside.

What would you think if you had gone to see a bed-ridden young girl who hadn't eaten or drunk anything for six years and when you turned up to see her she was out?

At that moment, an old lady accosted us, and my snapper chatted away to her in finest Portuguese – not a word of which I understood.

'She eats,' he said in the very worst broken English, demonstrating his words by putting his hand to his mouth.

'She's fucking gone to eat. But she's supposed to have been on a six-year starvation diet,' I shrieked.

What on earth am I going to tell PJ, I asked myself. Then I remembered there were no public phones in the village, so that was not going to be a problem until I got back to Oporto.

Now you might think that the Madonna's decision to pop out for lunch would end the *Sunday Mirror*'s interest there and then. But that couldn't be further from the truth. There was no way I was going home empty-handed. There must have been a reason why this girl was being hailed as a local saint.

We retired to a nearby bar – where else? – and I got him to start asking around the village about Maria. The message was crystal clear. She may have 'cheated' a little on the eating stakes, but on the whole she was a good sort of saint/Madonna and no one had a bad word to say about her. Then we had a lucky break. It turned out that the local paper had taken some photos of Maria in her traditional saint/Madonna pose, lying looking weak and hungry in bed at her home.

Forget the locals, forget Maria. We had to get round to the paper to buy those pictures, and fast! By this time my snapper and I had built up the sort of rapport normally reserved for monkeys and their trainers. But luckily he was fairly thick-skinned and took my swearing as a compliment.

The photos were great. Maria was clutching a crucifix as she lay, looking surprisingly happy despite her diet. The cheeks on her face were round and full and she looked as if she was a healthy three-meals-a-day sort of person, but I wasn't going to worry about mere details at that stage of the proceedings.

Thirty minutes later, we were twisting and turning on the treacherous mountain roads once more. This time I was far more relaxed, and I knew I had the story in the bag. The fact that we had never even met the girl didn't matter in the least. I had managed to interview the local paper journalist who had spoken to her, so I had plenty of quotes to use alongside her name. Most important of all, I had her photo.

By the time we got back to Oporto, I was cherishing the fact that I would never have to return to Tropeco ever again. It was hardly the kind of place that dreams are made of. The only obstacle now was my check-in phone call to PJ in London. This was a difficult one because I didn't know whether to tell him I hadn't actually interviewed the Madonna of the Mountains or just skim over the facts. After all, I had pictures and an interview, through the local paper reporter, so what was the point in telling PJ, I thought. I feared that he might send me back into the mountains and that seemed like a fate worse than death at that moment in time.

After half an hour of aborted attempts to get through to PJ, I finally made it. In the meantime I'd decided to take the coward's route and make out I had seen the girl. She was hardly going to get the *Sunday Mirror* in Tropeco, was she?

'Well done, mate. Brilliant!' came the usual enthusiastic response from PJ. Then there was a short silence at the other end of the line. I was aware that someone was talking to PJ in the office.

'Hello, PJ? Are you there?' I asked, intending to jolt him back into acknowledging my presence on the other end of the line.

'Yeah. Hang on a minute. Someone here is making a very good point about your story.'

I tried desperately to listen to what was being said but the line was cracking up and all I could hear were voices. I wondered what the hell they were all on about. I couldn't imagine what the matter was. It was all fairly simple, after all. Girl starves herself for six years after being visited by Christ. Can't get much simpler than that, can you?

'Wense?' Whenever PJ called me that I knew it meant trouble. 'Wense, did you manage to get a urine sample?'

This time the silence came from my end. Urine sample? What the hell is he on about?

'What do you mean, mate?' I asked incredulously.

'Well, if you don't get a urine sample, then how can we prove this girl isn't lying?' This was the man who was praised by the

Press Council for his conduct in the Lord Lambton affair speaking.

If she wasn't drinking she probably wasn't pissing, was my first thought. PJ had a fair point, but I wasn't going to admit it to him in a month of Sundays. And I certainly had no intention of going back up the mountains to try and persuade a seventeen-year-old girl to squat down and provide a total stranger with a bottle of her urine. In any case, I knew that would ruin the story. She had obviously broken her fast or else she would have died years earlier.

'But this is ridiculous, PJ. I can't expect her to co-operate with me, can I?'

I had broken one of the golden rules as far as PJ was concerned. I was being defeatist. The moment I'd said it, I knew it was a mistake.

'Well, I'm sorry, mate, but you're just going to have to go back to her and get a sample. Tell her we'll pay a hundred quid or something.'

Bloody marvellous, I thought, PJ always presumes that money will do the trick, but it's hardly going to mean much to a self-acclaimed saint. How the hell am I going to get out of this one? Another silence followed.

'But the stress might kill her, PJ.'

'Just get back out there and get a urine sample or don't bother coming back,' came the terse reply.

There was nothing else for it.

'PJ. I have got one thing and one thing only to say to you: why don't you piss off.'

At that I slammed the phone down, painfully aware that what I had just said would either get me the sack or be considered one of the wittiest off-the-cuff remarks ever made in Fleet Street history.

Ringing back five minutes later, I pretended it was a joke. But the truth was at the time I'd really meant it. Anyway, we both calmed down and I promised PJ I would try and get the girl to play ball over the piss-in-the-bottle request.

I did no such thing. I made no attempt to get in touch with

177

her and, instead, enjoyed a fine meal in an Oporto restaurant with my local snapper.

The next day I informed PJ of my failure to persuade the Madonna of the Mountains to give me a sample of her finest but, as was often the way with PJ, he had other things on his mind and didn't seem in the slightest bit bothered.

'Don't worry, mate. You've got enough to write it. Just get on the next plane home. I've got some real stories for you to cover back here.' It was typical PJ. After all that fuss . . . I vowed that if I ever got hold of the sod who suggested the urine sample, he'd be pissing in a bottle!

Mind you, the story that eventually appeared in the *Sunday Mirror* hid a multitude of journalistic sins. Headlined YEARS WITHOUT FOOD, it began:

The dark-haired teenager sits serenely in her snow-white bed and smiles . . . the quiet smile of a saint.

For a saint is what she is to thousands of pilgrims who flock to a mountain village in the north of Portugal.

Seventeen-year-old Maria Rosalina Viera says that Christ spoke to her over six years ago.

Since then she claims she has not eaten or drunk a drop of water.

Is the girl who should be dead a living miracle? Is she a saint? I visited Maria at her modest home in the village of Tropeco . . .

And so it went on.

I never interviewed her. I never saw her, but I still created a great read. It is amazing what you can achieve with a little luck and a little cunning.

I needed more than a little of that when I was sent, at about three-minutes' notice one Saturday morning in February 1982, to Vienna. The news had broken that very same day that film-star Richard Burton was divorcing his third wife Suzy, former wife of racing driver James Hunt. So what was all the fuss about? The answer comes in two simple words: Elizabeth Taylor.

For Burton's split from Suzy left the way open for one of the most glamorous film star couples of all time to rekindle their love. It was a marvellous tabloid opportunity to speculate about this glitzy romance but I sensed that I would need just as much Fleet Street expertise as I used in Portugal to cook up a decent story.

A measure of how important the *Sunday Mirror* considered the story was the fact they were sending me to Vienna on a Saturday morning with only hours to get a good story and file it in time for the next day's paper. By that late stage, the paper is normally full of stories that have been worked on throughout the previous week. It took national catastrophes to incite a News Editor to send a reporter abroad on a Saturday – or it took a story about Richard Burton and Elizabeth Taylor.

It is my idea of bliss to travel by plane at extremely short notice – that way I get less time to worry about hurtling through the air in a lump of old scrap metal. On top of that, being sent out at the eleventh hour meant I really had nothing to lose. If I got a good story, everyone would faint with admiration. If I failed, then the only person who'd get into trouble would be the News Editor for sending me out on such a crazy mission.

When I arrived at Vienna airport I knew exactly where I wanted to go – the luxurious Bristol Hotel in the city centre. That was where Burton and his entourage were staying during the filming of a TV movie on the life of composer Wagner. By the time my Mercedes taxi deposited me on the pavement outside the hotel, it was almost lunchtime. The minutes were ticking away towards deadline at six that evening. On arrival at the Bristol, I booked in and started my bid for an interview with Burton and co.

First of all, I tried an old and trusted trick that often gets a result when you need to find out a celebrity's hotel room number. I left a note addressed to Burton with the concierge in the hope that he would put it in the superstar's pigeon-hole. It worked like a dream. He was in room 152.

Next stage of my master plan was to establish who he had with him. It would have been sensational if he had had another girlfriend and she was staying in his suite. But it was not to be. A friendly bellboy revealed that he only had his personal assistant and one other assistant with him at the hotel. Also staying at the Bristol were the crew and actors from the film, but they were all out working on a scene that didn't require Burton's presence. There was a good chance that he would be alone in his suite. It was a perfect opportunity to try to talk to him.

My dilemma was this. Do I knock on Burton's door – or ring him on the internal phone – knowing that he is inclined to be dismissive of journalists, and so let him know I am here, with all the risks that that entails? Or do I try a softly softly approach to his assistant in an effort to get the clearance to have an official chat with Burton?

Sod it, I thought, I'll go and see him. I haven't got the time to fart around. I took the lift up to the first floor, literally shivering with expectation. This was my only chance and I knew it. Just a few seconds with Burton and I'd have enough for the front page. Do I pretend to be a hotel porter, or do I try a straight approach? One thing was for sure, my favourite PC Plod impression wasn't going to have much effect in the Bristol Hotel, Vienna. Fuck it, for once in my life I'll play it straight.

I tapped on the door gently. There was no reply. I knocked more forcefully.

'Yes. What is it?' came the gruff voice of our Welsh wonder from the valleys.

'Urgent message for you, Mr Burton,' I mumbled in an incoherent accent. It had taken me precisely ten seconds to give up the straight approach and try the deceptive method. What a relief. It's all so much easier.

'What message. Go away.'

Bloody hell! I've blown it already. I've got no choice but to steam in now.

'Hello, Mr Burton. My name is Clarkson. I am a journalist. I . . .'

'Go away,' was all my Hollywood hero would utter. The entire conversation had been conducted through a thick, dark wooden door. He hadn't even had the decency to show his face. It was all most unsatisfactory.

'But surely I could have a brief word, Mr Burton?'

No reply this time. That was it. The full extent of my interview with the Welsh wizard of the stage after travelling a thousand miles for the honour was ten words – an average of a hundred miles per word.

I walked back to the hotel reception area in a dejected mood. A totally new approach was required, so I decided to home in on the personal assistant, I rang her room and asked her if I could have a very urgent word with her. She came down and proved to be an absolutely charming, aunt-like figure who was obviously incredibly loyal to her illustrious charge.

However, she told me next to nothing. I was in trouble. It was three-thirty, and I had just ten meaningless words to file to London. I really couldn't see even the *Sunday Mirror* managing to make a front-page splash out of that.

Then I got chatting to a younger woman in the tearooms of the hotel as I munched my way through a delicious piece of Viennese chocolate cake. It turned out she was a friend of someone in the film crew and they'd all known about the divorce announcement for ages. I was getting somewhere at last. Then this young woman gave me a great line. She said she'd heard that Burton had taken a number of calls from Elizabeth Taylor in his hotel room earlier that same week. This was getting sensational. That old chestnut of Liz and Dick was back. It was just what I needed.

By four-thirty I was filing merrily away to London. The story appeared headlined: I CAN'T LIVE WITHOUT LIZ SAYS BURTON. It was a remarkably strong tale considering the indirectness of the source, but I was just happy to get something over to London. OK, so it came via a friend of a friend, but I wasn't revealing my sources.

But then that old bugbear of mine popped up to say hello – paranoia. After filing the story I started to get cold feet and terrifying thoughts went through my mind. What if the woman was making the whole thing up? What if she didn't even know a crew member, let alone the Burton entourage? I began to panic. It's a classic symptom of what's known in Fleet Street as 'pushing a story too far'. In other words, I'd got a little carried away with quoting un-named sources in my article. It is so easy to plant an extra quote or three in a story when the people you're quoting don't have names.

I knew I was guilty of doing that on this particular occasion, but it was too late to turn back. I could hardly ring P.J. Wilson back in London and say, 'Maybe that piece I just filed was a little bit over the top.'

I retreated to my room to await a call from London to say that all the first editions of the paper had been published. This normally happens at about eight on Saturday evening. If you were away on a big story you had to expect a call from the newsdesk to say what the others had on their front pages. The big worry was that they might have a better version of the story you had filed. On this occasion, I knew that was pretty unlikely to happen. I was more fearful that reporters would read my story and try to ring Burton or his sidekicks for confirmation. They would deny my article completely, I was sure.

Then, at about nine I got a knock at my door. I was convinced this was going to be trouble. It was a showbiz reporter from a rival daily paper who I knew was the only other British journalist in the hotel. He said to me: 'Well done. You've done a marvellous piece.'

I was speechless. The dodgiest story I'd ever filed in my life was being hailed as a masterpiece. I didn't pursue the subject with this particular journalist, instead we shared dinner together and talked about everything but Taylor and Burton. I was still feeling heavily guilty. By the end of the meal though, I had forgotten my troubles, thanks to a combination of fine wines and food.

Next day I flew back to London relieved to have got away with the whole episode. So far there had been no repercussions, and I was looking forward to getting home. But by Monday, the shit had really flown back in my direction. At least two papers ran a story claiming that Burton's eternal love for

Taylor was nonsense. I waited for the phone to start ringing. P.J. Wilson or the Editor were bound to start interrogating me. The Editor was particularly sensitive to adverse follow-ups to stories that appeared in his paper.

The call came. It was P.J. He just warned me to keep an eye on the dailies. Nothing more than that. It wasn't like him to be so relaxed, but then he wasn't the executive who'd sent me to Vienna. This time the shit didn't stop with him.

By now I was convinced I had pushed it too far and was about to get my come-uppance. When I walked into the office on Tuesday, P.J. Wilson started asking me what I thought of the Monday stories. I just laughed nervously and told him I wasn't worried. In truth I certainly was. I spent the rest of the day suffering from the worst bout of paranoia even I have ever endured. Each time the phone went on the newsdesk I thought it must be either the Editor to say he was sacking me or Richard Burton's solicitors to say he was suing me – or both!

I analysed every word PJ uttered into his phone, desperate to work out who he was speaking to. By the end of the day I was exhausted from nervous tension.

Then the most wonderful thing happened on the Wednesday evening. Elizabeth Taylor and Richard Burton met at a theatre in London. It was the best news of my life. To make matters even better, they spoke openly about their love for each other. I couldn't have been happier – or luckier – if I'd won the pools.

When I strolled into the office the next morning with the story blasted all over the front pages of the daily papers, I just felt like a hero. The Editor pulled me into his office to offer his congratulations, though I got the definite impression he was relieved my story had turned out to be true. PJ just laughed and winked at me. I tried to look serious, but the sense of relief on my face was there for everyone to see.

But maybe, in retrospect, it would have done me a hell of a lot more good if I'd been caught red-handed!

ELEVEN
Tiny Dick and the Big Cheque

THE CRUELLEST PERSONALITY CAREER OF ALL IS COMEDY. Comedians peak and then disappear with frightening regularity. One minute they're presenting their own Saturday-night special, the next minute they are miserable, withdrawn and heading for life's rubbish tip. Many comics, in any case, are sad people who put on a chirpy humorous front. More often than not, comedy is a tragic career that any normal person would do well to avoid. It's littered with failures and has-beens, and some say will continue to be so for as long as the good old British public carries on watching dismally unfunny television shows.

The reason I am making this deep and meaningful assessment is that this miserable type of humour was responsible for six of the most irritating weeks of my journalistic career. I know humour is a personal thing, but for me the very bottom of the comedy pit can be expressed in two words: – Dick Emery.

This tiny (in every sense of the word you can think of) little man had the infuriating habit of marrying a new wife on average about every couple of years. He also happened to be one of those painful slapstick comics whose BBC TV programme was watched by millions of brainless people every week. Unfortunately, in July, 1980, he decided to leave his fifth wife and I was assigned the odious task of signing him up for his life story.

'The Many Wives of Emery the Fifth,' yelled one newsdesk executive as he dispatched me post-haste for the so-called 'Town of the Stars', Weybridge in Surrey, where the little man and just about every other showbiz celebrity lived at that time.

'You've got the headline, now all you've got to get is 'im,' added my wise superior. The problem was that just about every other paper was after him, too. In those dark and distant days at the beginning of the last decade every tabloid reader was apparently just dying to know the secrets of the Casanova comedian and his womanising ways. Frankly, my impression of the so-called 'irrepressible little funny man' was that he was a raging queen, but more about that later. But as I drove down to the Millionaires' Paradise of Weybridge, I couldn't help asking myself how the hell this rather ordinary looking stand-up comic had managed to get through so many wives. I was shortly to find out the answer.

First stop was to be the Emery family home in deepest St George's Hills – the exclusive, celebrities-only district of Wey-bridge. It was always a golden rule on tabloids that if you were doing a marriage bust-up story the first port of call should be the embittered wife. She was always the one most likely to spill the beans and brand her hubby a variety of names that would do us very nicely, thank you. This time however, I wasn't really after the wife at all. I wanted to buy up Dick's life story but, as I had no other address at the time, I had to start there. It did not turn out to be a very impressive beginning to my involvement with the Emery marriage-go-round.

Wife number five, as she had already been called by every tabloid in town, was former dancer Josephine Blake. She had been swept up from the chorus line by Romeo Dick some years earlier, and had since matured into a formidable woman, as I was about to discover.

When I knocked on the door of the marital home – comparatively modest mock-Tudor detached job – she appeared in the regulation dark glasses that most showbiz types seem to insist on wearing if they are in mourning for a husband or wife lost through either death or divorce.

'I cannot possibly talk to you – go away.'

It was a perfectly understandable response, which I was naturally about to completely ignore.

'But your husband does seem to have a weakness for show-girls, Mrs Emery,' I said, knowing that he had run off with a blonde, younger version of herself. Please note that journalistic trick of calling people by their full title (Mr/Mrs/Sir/Your Lordship, Eminence, etc). It always makes them feel important. It also did the trick of prompting a reply from Mrs E.

'It was inevitable. He just cannot resist slender, long-legged looks,' she said in cool, calm, collected fashion. 'I could never see Dick falling for any girl who was not in showbusiness.'

That was it. She had said her piece. It was a pretty composed statement from a lady whose husband had just walked out on her for a younger woman – in fact it was delivered in such a calculated way that I kept looking for the script on the floor near the doormat.

I decided to push my luck a little further and asked: 'Where do you think your husband is living now?'

Mrs E looked through her Harrods sunglasses and me and replied: 'Try her family's home in Farnham.'

I was delighted to have scored such a notable success. After all, circumstances weren't ideal for obtaining this kind of information. I was relieved, too, that it was Farnham rather than Aberdeen or Hull. At least Farnham was just up the road. At this stage in my career at the *Sunday Mirror*, I had a reputation for finding people's addresses with little else but the name of their town to go by, so I was expecting to be sent in pursuit of this one. Sure enough, P.J. Wilson advised me to 'start digging around Farnham' for the house that Emery had turned into his secret lovenest.

It was mid-afternoon on a Friday, and like any healthy ambitious reporter I wanted to make sure I got a story in that Sunday's paper. It provided me with an added incentive to locate Emery's hideout fast and PJ knew that. And my Farnham mission was mercifully brief – thanks mainly to Dick Emery's fame. Everyone in Farnham thought they had seen our Dick in town. Some were actual sightings and some, without doubt, were the product of vivid imaginations. But the main thing was that I soon tracked down our unfunny little friend at a dull-looking detached mansion that very much resembled his former family home back in fascinating Weybridge. I recall chuckling at the fact that not only had he run off with a younger identikit version of his wife, but he'd even managed to end up in an identical house in a similar sort of stockbrokerish area.

The house, it turned out, belonged to Mrs Fay Hillier – the very same blonde showgirl whom our Dick had fallen for. She had, until a few weeks earlier, lived there with her own hubby, but he'd gone off on a trip abroad – rather considerately – and top TV funny man had moved in. As I crunched my way up the gravel driveway, I heard that most dreaded of distant sounds – the very distinguished bark of a big dog. It was difficult to tell if it was coming from inside or outside the house, so I marched on relentlessly and fearlessly – and if you believe that you'll believe anything! A number of rapid presses on the doorbell and aggressive knocks on the door revealed that no one was in. And the ravening beast was locked inside, luckily.

I was very depressed by this no-show on the part of our Dick and his blonde companion. I needed to sort his life story out quick, having only about twelve hours to file my piece, and I could have done without a tedious doorstep to increase the tension. But there was nothing else to do, so I sat in my car and began yet another wait in my long career of hanging around for people to come home. It had become second nature to me, but it was still fucking boring.

I was beginning to doze off when a Mercedes came swerving around the corner and took a left turn into the driveway. The driver looked like a transvestite in a red wig with aviator-style sunglasses. It was a bizarre sight to say the least. But there was one clue to whom 'it' might be – the attractive blonde sitting in the passenger seat. And we know who had a weakness for blondes, don't we?

Yes, it was our Dick in a ludicrous disguise. He was daft enough to think I wouldn't spot him. The greatest irony was that all the pack – who had apparently been in Farnham earlier in the week – had long gone and his amazing make-up had been laid on purely for the benefit of little old me.

But despite his slapstick attempt at avoiding the press, Dick was treating his own womanising ways as no laughing matter.

'Go away you horrible little man,' he shrieked at me.

Bloody cheek, considering he was about five foot three and I six foot one. Anyway, I took no notice and blasted forth at my victim:

'The *Sunday Mirror* would like to buy your life story for exclusive publication. There will be a very large financial reward involved.' So subtly put, don't you think?

Our Dick was definitely, if slowly, coming round to my way of thinking. 'How much?' he asked pointedly. 'I could do with the money.'

There was a grim, unhappy look on his face. It was my first insight into his total lack of a sense of humour.

'A lot of money, Mr Emery,' I replied dutifully, but thinking what an arsehole this man is. He must be worth a fortune but he's still not past haggling on the doorstep of his latest mistress's home.

'Speak to my agent,' he countered, pretending to only show a passing interest in my offer, while in fact very obviously being dead interested in it.

Bloody hell, I thought to myself. I've come all this way to be told to ring his agent. It was hardly the sort of result I wanted.

News Editor PJ was surprisingly happy when I called in. 'Don't worry, mate. Ring his agent and arrange a meet. I've got a feeling we may still get the bugger.' If only he'd known how appropriate that phrase was later to become.

By this stage on Friday evening, I had given up all hope of getting little Dick's life story in time for Sunday's paper, so I bashed out a news story based on wife number five's fantastic quote about how he could never resist a showgirl. The article made the top of page two of that week's *Sunday Mirror* – hardly a massive show, but at least it got my byline into the paper. But my pursuit of Dick's world-beating account of life in the showbiz fast-lane was still very much on the agenda. Over that weekend I contacted his agent and made all sorts of leading suggestions about how much cash might be available to Dick if he was prepared to make my day.

'But exactly how much money do you think the *Sunday Mirror* would be willing to offer, Mr Clarkson?' asked his agent.

'We're talking five figures here at least. Anything from £10,000 to £99,000, that is.'

'I think you'll have to be a bit more specific than that Mr Clarkson.'

It was clearly naive of me to think I could get away with such patter. The problem was that it had been drilled into me by certain executives at the *Sunday Mirror* NEVER to name the actual figure one was prepared to pay for a story. That way, if it came to the crunch and the Editor decided he only wanted to pay £10,000 rather than the £99,000 you'd been insinuating was on offer, the punter wouldn't be able to complain. The main aim of any tabloid is to suggest that his or her newspaper is going to pay the most loot. When it comes to dear old Joe Public, it usually works a treat. But showbiz agents (and certain bubbly blondes from Nottingham) are a different kettle of fish.

'*Can* you be more specific, Mr Clarkson,' said the agent, clearly well abreast of my dilemma.

'We have a particular figure in mind [a lie] but it is impossible to name that amount until we know exactly what Mr Emery is going to be prepared to talk about.'

I then went into one of my favourite spiels when caught in such a situation.

'It's a bit like going into a fruit and veg shop and buying a pound of apples without looking at them first to make sure they aren't covered in bruises.'

It was a line that nearly always worked, yet if you look at it closely, it makes no sense whatsoever. How many times have you managed to see every single apple in the bag you are buying? But at least it had the desired effect on our Dick's tough talking agent.

'I will come back to you Mr Clarkson,' he said.

There was no point in ringing my boss yet. I had to wait for the agent to ring back first. I didn't have to wait long.

'Mr Clarkson, you're in luck. I've just spoken to Dick and he says he'll talk to you about all five wives, Fay and everything else you want if the price is right.'

Now I was really cornered, and he knew it.

'I'll call you back within an hour with the actual figure.'

He had nailed me down to specifics now. No more apples. No more bullshit. I had to talk actual figures or else the deal would go up in smoke.

There was only one person to ring next and that was P. J. Wilson. As usual, I started the conversation in a very positive mode by telling him I reckoned we'd have Dickie baby 'signed up in time for next week'.

'How much money does he want?' asked PJ understandably.

'We haven't gone into specifics yet, but I gave him the old five-figure crap. The problem is PJ, he's already rung back to say that Dick will talk about the wives, the mistress, the lot, and I think I'll need to make an actual offer.'

There was a momentary silence at the other end of the line. If there was one thing PJ didn't like it was talking about specific sums of money in relation to stories.

'But we don't know what he's got to say yet . . . '

'I've already told him that load of old bollocks, and I told you, he's come back already to say what Emery will talk about. We've got to actually give him a figure, otherwise we'll lose it.'

I was really enjoying putting PJ under pressure for a change. If anything, I was acting more like Emery's agent than a reporter. But the truth of the matter was that I had learnt much of my art from PJ and he did sometimes tend to forget that fact. I also knew that the *Daily Mirror* – who had broken the story of Emery's fifth marriage problems in the first place – were desperate to get his life story for themselves. Despite being the daily version of the *Sunday Mirror*, they were rivals just like anyone else when it came down to the big buy-ups – and Dick Emery's tedious womanising came into that category. With this in mind, I warned PJ:

'The *Daily* is after this one in a big way. I've got a really good in with the agent [another lie since he was probably having problems remembering my name] so we've got to strike fast.'

This probably all sounds more like trying to contract Marlon Brando for a remake of *Gone With the Wind* than the pure and simple mechanics of getting a series of articles on a dull little grey-haired man into a tabloid newspaper. But that's the way it was (and still is).

It was now Monday, and I had spent most of the morning at home ringing the various characters involved in this saga. It was my day off (Sunday tabloids work Tuesday to Saturday) and I wanted to get the whole thing sorted out. Finally PJ caved in to the pressure and gave the reply I wanted.

'I'll talk to the Editor immediately and get him to tell me how much we'll pay. Gissa call back in half an hour and I'll have a decision.'

If only I had known what an annoying task I was about to undertake. All my boyish enthusiasm really was being channelled in the wrong direction on this occasion.

Just ten minutes later the phone rang once more.

'Hello, mate.' It was PJ. 'The Editor says we'll go thirty-five grand top whack.'

That was it. No more pleasantries were exchanged between the News Editor and myself and the line clicked dead. It was extraordinary, when you think about it. Here I was, being sanctioned to spend more money than the average worker earns in three years to a talentless comedian so he could tell me his life story.

But hang on. Note that expression 'top whack'. What it meant was: Try and get him to agree to half that amount, but if the worst comes to the worst, £35,000 is available.

Most reporters would have rung back the agent and started haggling from about £10,000. Not me. I knew the agent was as tough as nails and I was also aware from others that Emery was as tight as arseholes, so there was no point in beating around the bush. I also wanted to get the thing settled quickly because I was keen to secure the unusually large byline that always appears on these sort of kiss'n' tell type series.

'The editor personally says he is prepared to pay fifteen thousand,' I told the agent.

Ten minutes of telephone bartering later: 'OK, thirty-five thousand is a deal.'

The agent insisted on contracts being drawn up and signed

by all parties within twenty-four hours. He knew as well as anyone that my word wasn't worth the air I breathed to say it. It had to be in writing.

By the Tuesday lunchtime I was clutching the contract in my sweaty little palm having biked it half-way across London and the home counties in pursuit of Mr Emery's tired and weary signature. Remember that so far I had received little more than a torrent of abuse from him in a brief chat outside his Farnham lovenest. But now – thanks to the power of cash – I was about to share the innermost secrets of his life as Britain's randiest comic.

'Dick will meet you at the Star and Garter hotel in Farnham. He would rather you didn't go to his home,' said the agent when I rang to arrange a meet. How odd, you might well think, that a man who is about to be paid £35,000 to have a friendly chat doesn't want to meet up in the comfort and safety of his own home. The reason was, as I later discovered, more to do with the cost of food and drink than anything else. Just keep remembering the phrase 'tight as arseholes' and you should get the message.

Anyway, I was still going through my delighted stage at that time. I was over the moon that the deal had been signed, and I was dying to get on with it and write my first ever major feature series. This frame of mind survived all the way down to jolly old Farnham, but it was soon to die on meeting cuddly little Dick Emery.

But before that rendezvous could take place, I had to go through the sort of ritual normally associated with James Bond – or perhaps we are back in Inspector Clouseau territory. I had been instructed by the agent to go the reception at the hotel and book room twelve and then go up to the room and wait for Dickie baby to contact me. The hotel receptionist seemed to know all about it when I arrived.

'Mr Clarkson? Yes, your favourite room twelve has been prepared.'

Favourite room? I had never been to the hotel before in my life, but I wasn't about to shatter all this suspense by telling her.

Tiny Dick and the Big Cheque

It seemed odd but harmless all the same, so I didn't let it worry me.

Room twelve was in fact exceedingly dull. There were no showgirls, not even a water bed and, even more annoying than that, there was no Dick Emery.

Five minutes later the phone rang and a slightly effeminate man's voice asked: 'Is that Mr Clarkson?' There was only one reply that I could give. 'This is Emery here. I'll be with you in half an hour.' *Click.* The phone went dead. To say I sat nervously awaiting my brand new best friend would have been an overstatement. I was just a bit puzzled by all the cloak-and-dagger stuff. Was it really all that necessary?

There was a knock on the door thirty minutes later, and in strolled this short, quite dapper (in a bank manager sort of way) little man in early old age. There was a look of what I can only describe as jolly tension on his face.

'Hello there. I've only got a couple of hours so you'd better get on with it.'

It was businesslike to the point that he sounded more like a call girl about to earn her crust in a hotel bedroom than a top comedian. He may have sparked off week after week of canned laughter in those BBC studios, but he was hardly having me chuckling in the aisles now.

'Oh, you're much younger than I expected.' His voice had changed into that of one of those tiresome fishwives he used to characterise on telly. The problem was that it had a completely different effect when uttered by a besuited old chap in a Farnham hotel. He sounded like a raging queen, the kind who only looks at a woman in order to imitate her. It was not an encouraging start to the proceedings.

Small talk over, I launched in to the subject at hand. I soon discovered it was not going to be easy. He may have been about to receive £35,000, but it didn't seem to be having the desired effect on his interview technique. A typical exchange between us went something like this:

'Tell me, Dick. You've had a lot of women in your time, but who was the real love of your life?'

'I'd rather not tell you.'

'What was it that first attracted you to your current girlfriend Fay?'

'I can't remember.'

'Is it true that you can't resist showgirls?'

'I don't know. Is it?'

Things were not going well between Dick and me, and we'd already been talking for half an hour. You can always tell when a disaster looms if the subject starts answering questions with questions. But this wasn't some doorstep on a naive punter, this was a pre-agreed deal worth thirty-five grand. I was stumped. I was getting fucking nowhere and I didn't know what to do. In normal circumstances it would seem reasonable to expect the subject to be co-operative when they are being paid a huge sum. But not, it seemed, our Dickie.

After a further thirty minutes of getting nowhere fast, I made my excuses and left the room. I headed straight for the phone in the hotel lobby and rang PJ.

'He won't open up properly,' I said to PJ in what was probably the understatement of the week.

'Tell him he won't get the bloody money if he doesn't co-operate,' replied PJ. I could tell the way he was thinking. He would look a right idiot if he had to tell the Editor that the Emery buy-up was off because the comic wouldn't say anything. But I knew that if I got aggressive with our Dick he would probably storm out, and that would get us nowhere.

Then PJ – probably following my train of thought – added: 'You'll get it all out of him. Take your time and get him a bit sloshed. He's probably feeling a bit tense and nervous.'

With that I put the receiver down and headed straight for the hotel bar, from where I rang room twelve. Earlier, I had told him there was something wrong with the phone and I was going down to order some sandwiches as an excuse to get out and ring PJ. Dick wasn't the cleverest of people so he didn't question the phone's miraculous recovery when he answered it.

'I thought I'd get some drinks in. What would you like, Dick?'

'A scotch would be very nice,' came the camp reply.

Three minutes later, I appeared at room twelve with a full bottle of Johnny Walker, two glasses and some ice. Dick's eyes lit up. At last I had found his weak spot. I poured a quadruple whisky for him without ice and a double for me with ice to make it last longer. At this pace, I reckoned it would take at least an hour to get him to open up. I was about right.

It all began to come out. A brief lowdown on each of the five previous wives; how he had started in showbusiness; his attitudes to women in general. But God it was boring. All his answers were stilted and totally lacking in colour, but at least he'd started to crack.

By nine o'clock that evening we were both shattered and agreed to reconvene the next day. Dickie baby was hardly able to stand up. No wonder he'd picked a hotel such a short distance from his lovenest. Luckily, I was able to just flop straight into bed, but I waited until I was sure Dick had departed from the premises. I was still most unsure about him. That was a minor worry compared to the fact that I knew Emery's interview was fucking boring, even when one considered the subject matter. However, the whisky prevented me from agonising too deeply, and I fell asleep with ease.

Next day was much the same except that little Dickie had somehow warmed to me. I wasn't sure whether that was such a good thing. In between talking about his prowess with women, he would continually pat me on the leg and say: 'Oh Wensley, I wish I had a son like you.'

It was hardly a situation I relished. Even I, one of Fleet Street's pushiest, drew the line at certain things when it came to making sacrifices to get a story. Here I was, sitting on the edge of a double bed in a hotel room in Farnham with a camp old gent patting my knee and telling me what a nice boy I was. I began pouring yet more whisky down his gullet.

But despite his fondness for me, he still wasn't giving me what I really wanted. It was becoming more and more obvious that the man didn't have an interesting thought in his head. He had spent the previous thirty years using a script or a tele-prompter and the results, from my point of view, were disas-trous. He just couldn't string an entertaining sentence together.

By the end of the second session I was getting desperately worried that the material I had was useless from a tabloid point of view. But in his own eyes, Dick believed he was giving me just what I wanted. Thank God he never actually tried to give me anything else.

Throughout all this I had avoided admitting to P.J. Wilson that there had been any setbacks other than the initial teething problems. When I walked into the office the next morning to begin bashing out the amazing three-part series on the life and loves of Romeo telly comic Dick Emery, I was a worried man.

Six hours later I had handed in the first part of the series to an executive in charge of that part of the paper. Within five minutes he was on the internal phone to my desk.

'This is fucking boring crap. It's not worth thirty-five pee, let alone thirty-five grand.'

He was only telling me what I already knew. But one of my problems was that the Editor had insisted the series be written in the first person, like an autobiography. Every word had to grab your attention, yet all Dick had managed through me was this sort of thing: 'I always liked going out with women. Even from an early age I used to enjoy their company.' Whereas what the *Sunday Mirror* wanted (and needed to help their circula-tion) was something like: 'Every time I see a girl I want to make love to her. I've got an insatiable appetite for sex.'

The esteemed executive continued: 'Go back to Emery and spell out the facts. If he wants the money, then he's got to play the game.'

But having just spent two nervous days with the so-called zany genius of the small screen, I knew he'd never provide that sort of material. Any normal business faced with a problem like this would simply cancel the contract and drop the whole idea. Not tabloids. No way. The *Sunday Mirror* wanted that series, and I was going to have to provide what they wanted. I knew that. I just had to work out how I could deliver the goods.

I examined the options available. They didn't make good reading:

1. I go back to Emery and start all over again.

2. I tell my bosses it will never work and the series must be dropped.

3. I re-write the whole series and then try to persuade Emery to sign each piece of copy to make sure there are no come-backs afterwards.

The first two options were out of the question. Number three was the only plan available. But I was playing a dangerous game, and I knew it. Persuading Dick Emery to sign the copy was going to be a nightmare, since it would hardly contain a word he'd said. Also, I was sure he would make a complaint afterwards and that would look bad for me. All the same, I sat down at my desk and started to make up the whole feature series. Here is a fine example:

Dick's original copy ran: 'She was a very nice looking girl and I found myself most attracted to her.'

My brand new version read: 'She was a real corker and I fancied her like crazy.'

Basically, I had awarded myself full poetic licence to do what I wanted to make sure the articles worked. After the first few pages I started to enjoy myself and get even more carried away:

Dick's original version: 'I couldn't help noticing her figure.' My version: 'I saw her and thought "Cor blimey, I'd like to get my hands on that." '

I knew that our readership would be expecting Dick's words to read like those of some of the pathetically unfunny characters he played on his TV show. That was precisely how I was writing his material.

In next to no time I had re-written the whole three-part series. But the next stage in this elaborate sting was going to be considerably more difficult. I had to pop down to Farnham and explain all to Uncle Dickie. Not an easy task, I feared.

To make matters even more tense, it was Friday morning and I had to deliver the completed series by no later than the end of that day. I have to admit I was not feeling particularly happy as I sped towards a make-or-break meeting at Farnham's highly unimpressive Star and Garter. All I had told little Dick on the phone earlier was that I needed him to sign the articles to make sure 'we are all happy with the contents'. I knew it would turn out to be somewhat more complex than that. Things started ominously when I arrived at the hotel and found that room twelve was not available. I never worked out why Dickie baby was so fond of this particular room. As usual I feared the worst and convinced myself it was because he had used it for purposes other than sleep, but he was too canny to reveal all when I probed him on this point.

I settled for room eleven, and just hoped he wouldn't throw a wobbly because I hadn't got his favourite room. Before going up to the room I ordered the traditional full bottle of Johnny Walker, two glasses and just enough ice for me. My masterful game plan was to stuff as much scotch down his gob as quickly as possible. I just kept repeating to myself: 'He's got to sign. He's got to sign.'

Eventually he showed up, looking even more harassed than usual. It wasn't the sort of mood I wanted him to be in, but there was no turning back.

'I really need one,' was tiny Dick's reply when I offered him a drink. This at least was encouraging. He knocked it back in one and I slowly began to regain confidence in what I was doing.

Then he did it again: 'Oooooooh. You do remind me of my son. I do wish he was a writer like you.'

It was the twentieth time he'd brought the conversation round to me in the past four days. The hand then slapped my thigh affectionately. All I could think to myself was: If only you knew what I've written on your behalf you wouldn't be so fond of me.

Now was not the moment to spring such surprises on my mini friend, so I let him carry on with his affectionate patter – just so long as it stayed on a harmless level. As he rambled on some more about how he wished I was his son, I began to wonder what the fuck I would do if he really tried it on with me. I was getting nervous. Not only was I about to try and get him to put his signature to forty pages of wild exaggeration, but I was going to have to rebuff his sexual advances.

But it never happened. In fact, I think it was more paranoia on my part than sexual desire on his. The hand never went further than a friendly pat on the thigh, and later I felt a bit guilty at being so homophobic. However, I was still nowhere near getting my somewhat fictional story signed and sealed. Dick was still reminiscing about the good old days as the whisky bottle got emptier and emptier. I knew I just had to wait for the perfect moment.

By now, he seemed much more relaxed than when he had first arrived that day. The drink had really done the trick. I decided I needed to get him so pissed that he would be barely able to read the copy. But on the other hand he had to be sober enough to scratch his signature at the bottom of each of the forty sheets of A4 paper.

'Dick,' I feigned a slur so he would think I was as drunk as him. 'I've got the copy here and I wonder if you could just initial it for me.'

Much easier for him to stick his initials on each sheet rather than go through all the effort of writing his own name. Dick looked as if he didn't have a care in the world at that moment. He must have been thinking it was going to be the easiest £35,000 he'd ever earned in his life.

'Sure, Wensley. Anything for you sweetheart,' came the reply.

Then I remembered that my copy lacked one thing that was essential to Dick's life story as one of Britain's best-loved comics – his favourite joke. I thought I might as well get that off him before I hit him with the bombshell of the fictitious articles.

'Actually Dick, there is one thing I needed to ask you before we go through the copy,' I explained thoughtfully. 'I am certain that all our readers would love to know what your favourite gags are.'

Now, you would think that was a perfectly reasonable request to make of a comedian, wouldn't you? Dick definitely didn't see it that way. A sort of puzzled look came over his face. He seemed distinctly uncomfortable.

'My favourite gags?'

'Yes, that's right, Dick. You must know thousands of them,' I enthused. I sensed that this was the beginning to turn into a major manoeuvre. At least two minutes of silence followed. The suspense was killing me. I presumed that Dick was mentally sifting through those thousands of cracking gags that he never got round to telling on his TV show. I didn't dare say anything in case it ruined his concentration.

Finally, he turned to me and said with a completely straight face: 'I can't really think of any at the moment. Why don't you ring my agent and ask him?'

Fuck me! This was a story in itself: TOP COMEDIAN CAN'T THINK OF A JOKE!

'But,' I said, rather stupidly in the circumstances, 'don't you know one good one, Dick?'

He looked furious. In his case, this was worse than questioning his already doubtful manhood.

'No, I bloody well don't. I've told you. Ring my agent.'

All that fine work with the whisky bottle had gone to waste in one foul-up. I should have known better.

In a rather feeble attempt to defuse the situation, I reassured him: 'Don't worry. It's no great problem.'

But the damage had already been done. Rather than try and get him to put his initials to my copy there and then, I decided the only thing to do was ring the agent immediately and allow him a few minutes to relax while I was on the phone. So there I was, sitting in a hotel room with Britain's most famous TV comic, phoning his agent to ask him what his client's favourite jokes were. The answer was a handful of such poor gags that I replaced them with one of my own jokes when I got back to the office later that night.

Anyway, it had the desired effect of diverting little Dick's anger, which was really a disguise for his embarrassment. Now it was back to the very much harder task of getting him to agree to the lies I had written about him.

'Here's all the copy, Dick. Why don't you cast your eyes over it and then sign it. I am a bit pushed for time.'

I deliberately made out I had to get back to the office because I wanted him to skim through the copy so quickly that he wouldn't notice all the inaccuracies. I had even, slimily, made sure that the first ten pages were pretty close to what he had told me. I wanted him to feel an (entirely false) sense of security so he wouldn't bother reading it all. I poured him out another huge scotch but became more concerned when he left the glass on the table as he put on his reading glasses and started to make a frighteningly sober-looking effort to concentrate. This was not what I wanted to happen.

For at least ten minutes he said nothing. He was reading very slowly and deliberately. But he hadn't got past the first ten pages of smokescreen yet. By now, I was the one doing the drinking. I was shitting hot bricks – no two ways about it. If he threw a fit and refused to sign, the whole fucking project would crumble, and my career with it. I would look a complete moron. At last Dickie baby looked up at me over the top of his reading glasses. He had gone a puce colour and was quivering.

'You've made all this up. I didn't say a word of it. I am not signing any of this garbage. Go away and come back with what I told you – not these lies. You've made me look a complete idiot.'

It was the most truthful statement to come between us throughout our four days of meetings, but it didn't help things at that moment. There was no time left. I *had* to get him to sign.

'I'm sure we can sort all this out. Tell me where the inaccuracies are, Dick,' I said hopefully.

'Inaccuracies? None of this is true. I never say things like "Cor blimey, she was a bit of all right." It makes me look a right prat.'

Many a true word . . . I thought to myself, but felt it inappropriate to point it out at that moment. The whisky bottle was still more than half full, and it was definitely time to change the subject, get more pissed, and then try the gentle art of persuasion once again. It was going to be a long day.

'Let's run through it all slowly and I'll point a few things out to you,' I said, as I filled his glass practically to the rim.

We started on page one, and I countered every accusation of inaccuracy with the same defence: 'Look, Dick, it just sounds much livelier than what you said, but it *means* exactly the same thing.'

At first he wasn't having any of it.

'That's crap and you know it.'

'But it's still accurate, Dick. I've just put it in a different way that suits the *Sunday Mirror* style.'

After a solid hour of toing and froing, we were still at each other's throats. If only he'd meant all that earlier stuff about how he wished I'd been his son. All that sentimental crap had long since gone. He wasn't even patting my thigh any more. I was beginning to miss it.

There comes a time during negotiations like these when you realise you have got to take a risk and get tough. Dick Emery was being paid £35,000 to tell his life story in the *Sunday Mirror*. But he'd told his story in a very boring way. It had to be spiced up. He was getting a fortune, so he should just shut his mouth and take the money.

Rapidly coming round to this way of thinking I said firmly to Dick: 'Look, mate. You either want thirty-five grand or you don't.'

He looked stunned. I had the whisky to thank for my outburst, but I knew it was the only way out. This was a man who had four wives (one had died) to support.

'OK. You've made your point. Write what the hell you want. I'll sign all this and then you can leave me in peace,' he said through gritted teeth.

I am afraid to say that I didn't feel so much as a twinge of guilt at the time. This bloke was getting paid a fortune for basically fuck all. He had no right to complain – in fact I was doing him a huge favour.

That Sunday, and for the following three weeks, a series of two-page articles appeared in the *Sunday Mirror* with a variety of spicy headlines like: I AM UNSTOPPABLE ONCE I FANCY A GIRL, and HOW I TRAIN FOR LOVE. My mission had finally been accomplished.

I only spoke to Dick Emery once again. It was about a year later and, surprise, surprise, he had split up with leggy girlfriend Fay. This time there were no more showgirls to run to. Instead, he moved into a little flat in London on his own and told me, rather pathetically, 'I'm just a lonely old man now.' What a difference a year makes.

Then I had a peculiar experience shortly after he died a couple of years later.

A contact of mine inside his agent's office telephoned me just after Dick's cremation service to tell me about an extraordinary tussle that was going on between Emery's widow (wife number five – they never divorced) and his mistress, Fay Hillier. It turned out that these two women were in serious dispute about who had the right to keep our Casanova comic's ashes. Fay had grabbed the urn after the service and placed dear old Dick on the mantelpiece of the couple's modest new lovenest in Shepperton. The shapely, long-legged ex-dancer was determined to hold on to her beloved Dick.

Then mourning widow Josephine, forty-three, demanded that she should have them. An almighty row ensued. Somehow, in circumstances that were never fully explained, the urn ended up at the mansion in Weybridge where Josephine still lived.

Poor old Dick. In his will he asked for his ashes to be scattered on the Thames, but the funeral directors had put the kibosh on that little idea by announcing it would constitute a health hazard. Now he was spending his time locked up in a silver urn travelling to and fro between respectable Weybridge and equally civilised Shepperton. It was hardly the sort of ending he had in mind. To be honest, it was an unbelievably tacky situation, and when I told my News Editor he found it difficult to believe. But my tip came from an impeccable source, as they say in the trade, so off I went to Weybridge in search of Dick Emery's ashes.

At the mock-Tudor mansion, Josephine was furious. She refused to open the door to me. I felt like saying: 'Is Dick there?' but I resisted the temptation. After all, he was sitting in an urn on the mantelpiece minding his own business.

So, Josephine had finally got her husband back and, unlike three years earlier, there was no need for her to re-direct me to a lovenest in Farnham. All the same, I couldn't help feeling a touch of déjà-vu as I hurtled across Surrey to talk to his mistress about how the wife had got hold of his ashes. It was just like old times again. But not even a comedy scriptwriter (unlike Dick's own team of word-slaves) could have created this sort of scenario.

Strangely enough, Fay was just as reluctant to talk. I don't think she had ever forgiven me for persuading Dick to sign the 'world exclusive' that we ran as a feature series after his marriage break-up.

But my newsdesk weren't going to give up that easily. They had me steaming the eight or nine miles between mistress and wife and back again for the next twenty-four hours. I began to get an insight into how poor old Dick must have felt inside that urn. Part of the problem was that myself and my colleague working on the story for the *Sunday Mirror* were not taking the task at hand entirely seriously. Would you?

By the time I was about to knock on the widow's home for the third time to ask her if little Dick was still sitting on the mantelpiece, I could hold myself back no longer. As I waited for her to answer, I burst into an uncontrollable fit of laughter. I couldn't stop myself. Not surprisingly, it rapidly became infectious and my colleague joined in. Within seconds we recognised the potential danger of the situation and retreated to our staff car at the end of the gravel driveway.

Picture the scene: Grieving widow comes to door and two tabloid hacks start to ask about husband's ashes and then start howling with laughter. Subsequently they beat a mirthful retreat.

Tiny Dick and the Big Cheque

We carried on sniggering in the car for at least twenty minutes, while Josephine looked around her premises trying to work out who had just rung her front door-bell and run off. Hopefully she thought it was a gang of bloody kids.

Then it was back to the mistress's HQ at picturesque Shepperton by the Thames. Pretty much the same thing happened there. This time there was no driveway to retreat down, so we ran off to a pub up the road instead. Needless to say, a couple of pints didn't help ease our spasms of hilarity.

We both had finally managed to curtail – or so we thought – our humour levels when we drove back to Weybridge for one last crack at widow Jo. As we cruised through the town's high street, I spotted the unmistakable figure of the grieving widow walking into Woolworths. It was a fantastic opportunity to talk to her – so much easier to interview your prey out in the open than through a mock-Tudor style front door. I screeched to a halt and we both jumped out like something out of *Streets of San Francisco*. With my nose I had to be Karl Malden.

How could I be so sure it was indeed the widow in question? Simple. She was still wearing the same Harrods sunglasses she'd worn the day I first called at her house to ask about her marriage break-up three years earlier. I told you they were standard showbusiness uniform in times of mourning for a husband or wife lost through death or divorce.

Anyway, I told my partner – he'd better be Michael Douglas – to stand guard at the entrance to Woolworths, while I tried to smoke her out. I decided not to confront her at first. I just wanted to make sure she didn't slip out of the store and into the thronging crowds. For ten minutes I watched and waited as she inspected almost every item in the Woolies underwear section. It was not a pleasant experience – housewives were beginning to wonder what a Karl Malden nose-alike was doing sniffing (I had a cold at the time) around shelves filled with rather plain looking women's knickers. Widow Jo still hadn't cottoned on to my little spying game. She must have been the only person in Woolworths who hadn't.

Meanwhile, Michael Douglas at the front door was getting

twitchy. He wasn't particularly worried. It was just that he had broken into yet another uncontrollable fit of laughter. People were walking past him and wondering if he was a nutter.

Blissfully unaware of this scene, I decided to follow Josephine out into the street and then pounce. When, after much deliberation, she invested in two pairs of Woolies finest 100% cotton knickers, I knew that moment was fast approaching. But, as she sauntered through the heavy glass swing-doors, I noticed a crowd had gathered. They were looking at a man lying on the pavement. 'I think he's had a fit,' said one helpful onlooker. 'Better get a doctor, quick,' said another.

I glanced briefly down at the sidewalk, anxious not to lose my quarry, and there, with tears of laughter rolling down his cheeks, was my partner. He had collapsed in a heap because the giggling fit had proved too much. What a dilemma. I didn't know whether to take care of my colleague or hare after Jo. I stopped quickly by the quaking body on the pavement, decided he had just caught another bout of hysterics, and turned on my heel to pursue Josephine down Weybridge High Street.

It was too late. She had disappeared into the crowds, happily ignorant of the fact that I now knew what her latest pair of knickers looked like. So I returned to my colleague. But it was hopeless. I caught the laughter bug as well. It started with light giggles. Then serious guffaws developed. Finally, I too was incapacitated.

I don't suppose Weybridge will ever see the like again.